THE JOY OF
KEEPING THE FAITH

Thriving in the Church
after RCIA

CHRISTINE WAY SKINNER

© 2020 Novalis Publishing Inc.
Cover design: Jeff McCall
Cover image: ©Shutterstock.com / melitas
Layout: Audrey Wells

Published in Canada by Novalis
Publishing Office
1 Eglinton Avenue East, Suite 800
Toronto, Ontario, Canada
M4P 3A1
www.novalis.ca
ISBN: 978-2-89688-443-8

Head Office
4475 Frontenac Street
Montréal, Québec, Canada
H2H 2S2

Cataloguing in Publication is available from Library and Archives Canada

Published in the United States by
TWENTY-THIRD PUBLICATIONS
One Montauk Avenue, Suite 200
New London, CT 06320
(860) 437-3012 or (800) 321-0411
www.twentythirdpublications.com
ISBN: 978-1-62785-516-7

Printed in Canada.

We acknowledge the support of the Government of Canada.

5   4   3   2   1   24   23   22   21   20

CONTENTS

INTRODUCTION

Keep the Faith

Keep the faith! When I was a child, we had a parish priest; Father Walter Healey was his name. "Keep the Faith" was his motto. This saying appeared regularly in the bulletin, in cards he wrote to people and, at the end of his days, on the cover of the program for his funeral Mass. Father Healey's use of this phrase affected me so much that I still remember him doing it forty years after the fact. If truth be told, I always found it a bit odd. It seemed like basic common sense to me – like "be safe" or "drive carefully!" Why would anyone even consider the alternative of *not* being safe, *not* driving carefully or *not* keeping the faith? To do otherwise is to risk one's life. It didn't make sense to me. But I still rather liked that he always used the phrase.

Now, these forty years later, I have a different perspective. As my dad was fond of saying, "Common sense isn't really all that common." People do not always make safe choices, drive carefully or, even, keep the faith. We continue to remind one another to do the things we need to do to live our lives. In our loving care for one another, we continue to call each other to common sense. So, it is a perfect phrase to offer you, a new Catholic. Whether you have just been baptized or have joined the Catholic Church from a different tradition, it is now up to you to "keep the faith" that has been entrusted to you as a gift and that you have chosen to accept. In so doing, you will guard your spiritual life just as by driving carefully you will guard your physical life.

I didn't know it at the time, but "keep the faith" wasn't Father's phrase. It came from St. Paul. In his letter to Timothy, Paul reflected on his life and told Timothy he believed that he had been a faithful servant of God. He wrote, "I have fought the good fight, I have kept the faith." (2 Timothy 4:7) As a new Catholic, you are likely full of hope that you, like St. Paul, will continue to fight the good fight and keep the faith. And we, companions in this Church you have joined, hope and pray the same for you. As part of our commitment to support you, we offer you this series of reflections and advice.

This book is not intended for directors of initiation, pastors or catechists, though they might find it helpful. It is written for you, the neophyte, now beginning the practice of your faith in this Church founded by Christ Jesus. You have been through a lengthy process of discernment, preparation and initiation. You have had guides and teachers and other candidates and catechumens with whom you have met regularly. But you no longer have the regular companionship of an initiation team and other candidates and catechumens. It is time to launch. The advice in this book is intended to help you navigate the next phase of your faith journey.

Faith that Fizzles – Faith that Flourishes

As a director of Christian initiation for most of my professional life, I have seen many people enter the Church. These people have come with a wide range of **knowledge** of the Church. Some are very familiar with the faith. One woman I worked with had been attending Mass with her husband since they had met more than thirty years before our meeting. She had raised a Catholic family, participated in most parish events and knew Church teaching better than some cradle Catholics. Everyone assumed she was Catholic. On her twenty-fifth wedding anniversary, she came to my office and told me she had decided that it made sense to join the Church to which she, functionally at least, already belonged.

Other people, however, arrive on the doorstep of the church with no knowledge of even the basic Christian beliefs. They have been raised in a non-religious family in a non-Christian culture. But they are looking for something to make sense of their lives, and what they have seen of the Catholic Church appeals to them.

People also come with a wide range of **commitment**. For some, the inquiry process has been going on informally for years, and their search for the Living God has been intense and intentional. Others come wanting their children to be placed in the Catholic school system and, admittedly, are not interested in practising the faith in any committed fashion.

Those who enter the process of initiation in the Roman Catholic Church also come from all conceivable **demographics** of gender, race, culture, age, and economic and professional backgrounds. In my own ministry, I have worked with people as young as seven (the lower limit for this process) to as old as eighty-eight. The latter was a wonderful quiet and wise Jamaican woman named Etta, who brought Jamaican rum punch to our gathering when it was her turn for treats and who recently passed away at the age of 105 and a half years. I have seen lawyers, business people, social workers, teachers, plumbers, musicians, people who are unemployed and even a woman who practised prostitution choose to join this Church of more than a billion members.

What this diverse group of people had in common is that they had faith at least the size of a mustard seed and wanted to find support for living that faith in and from the Catholic community.

The faith of most people who have been through the process of initiation has flourished. Some have become pillars of parish life, taking on important roles of service in the community. When I look out on any given Sunday, I see lectors, choir members, ministers of hospitality and members of the finance council who once sat in my office wondering if God might be calling them to become Catholic. However, for some, sadly, their faith has fizzled. For one reason or another, they have left the Church and never returned. I have remained in contact with many of these people (those who have stayed and those who have not). I have listened to their insights about faith as time has passed. I have also made some observations of my own. This book is a sharing of those insights about what has helped people to "keep the faith." Some of these insights come directly from people who, like you, have been through the initiation process. These are found in boxed quotes throughout the book.

Wherever *you* have come from or whatever has brought *you* here, we hope that your faith will flourish and that you will find the place in the Christian community that God has carved out for you. You, the Church and the world will be richer if this happens.

The Parable of the Sower

The success or failure of the Gospel message taking root in us is not a new problem. Indeed, Jesus saw that when he preached, his words were received in a variety of ways. Sometimes, the Word took hold and flourished. In other instances, it did not. Jesus saw a parallel between the growth of seeds and the growth of faith. In his typical fashion, he told his disciples a parable to explain this growth. He spoke about a sower who sowed seed on the ground. Some of the seed fell on the path but was trampled on or eaten by birds. Some fell on rocky ground and dried up. Some seed fell among weeds which choked it. But some of the seed fell on good soil and became fruitful.

As commonly as Jesus told parables, the disciples did not understand them. So, Jesus went on to explain that the seed was like God's Word. Some people receive the Word but, like a seed that is not planted in good soil, it is vulnerable. The seed is "stolen" by those who speak words that are easier to hear or less challenging to live but are not ultimately life-giving. These are words spoken by lesser powers, by devils, as it were. Sometimes the seed takes root quickly but superficially. The first signs of growth bring great joy, but because those signs are superficial, they cannot bear the test of time or the challenge of the elements. Sometimes the seed is overwhelmed by weeds. (As a gardener, I most relate to this part of the parable.) The "cares and riches and pleasures of life" take over, and the seed cannot compete and dies. Jesus encourages us, however, to hear the Word and to "hold it fast in an honest and good heart." If we do so, with patient endurance, we will be like good soil and that Word will bear fruit.

You can find this parable in the Gospel of Luke (8:4-18). I encourage you to read it and to reflect on it regularly in your prayer as you work to ensure that your new-found faith develops strong roots and continues to deepen and grow so it can withstand the challenges that you, like every Christian, will inevitably face.

The question now is, how do we ensure that the Word you have heard finds fertile soil so that it takes root and provides bountiful fruit?

The Non-Negotiables

Seeds have some absolute needs: sunlight, water, fertilizer. These are non-negotiables. Without them, the seed doesn't have a chance. Faith is similar. If faith is going to flourish, some practices are non-negotiable. Without these practices firmly in place, our faith will not have the strength to withstand the first challenge. We will be like those people who receive the Word with joy but because it takes no root, it cannot be sustained. Here are the non-negotiables of faith:

1. Place God at the centre of your life.
2. Develop a practice of personal prayer.
3. Live liturgically.
4. Participate in the life of the Church community.
5. Put faith into practice.
6. Find ways to support ongoing learning and spiritual growth.

Within these non-negotiables, the Catholic Church offers a wide variety of ways in which you can find just the right way of practising your faith to fit your personality, culture and individual circumstance. Let us now look at these important aspects of strong and mature faith in more depth.

I

BUILDING A HOUSE ON SOLID ROCK – PLACING GOD AT THE CENTRE

In the Gospels of Matthew and Luke, Jesus reminds us that a strong faith needs a strong foundation. (Matthew 7:24; Luke 6:48) Living faithfully is comparable to building a house. If we build our house on sand, at some point it will collapse and wash into the sea. If we want our house to last, it must be built on a solid foundation – a rock-solid foundation. Only rock will hold up our house against the elements. The Rock on which we need to build our Christian life is God. God alone will hold us up. God alone will not disappoint.

Whatever drew you to the Church in the first place – Grandma's constant rosaries, Father Friendly's warm welcome, Sister Scholastica's intellectual challenge, a longing for community, the search for a sense of purpose, an attraction to the beauty of worship, the desire to be of the same faith as your spouse and children – only God will keep you here.

The most common reason I see for the fizzling of the practice of faith is that the person's faith was not really, fully and deeply in God, experienced through his Son Jesus Christ and strengthened by the Holy Spirit. Instead, the Church was chosen because of individual relationships with people, a sense of community or some other noble but ultimately fallible thing. When these things failed the believer in a substantial way, membership in the Church was abandoned. This is true for cradle Catholics as well as those who are newly initiated.

Have Faith in God but Be Patient with the Rest of Us

While it is important to have faith and trust in those we love, the Church and our religious leaders, it is God alone who is worthy of worship. Our spouses, our children, our friends and even the Church reflect God's goodness, love and care for us… but they reflect it imperfectly.

Marriages break down. If your reason for joining the Church was unity with your spouse, and your reason for staying remained this, then often a marriage failure means the end of the practice of faith. Our spouses, no matter how much we love them, will fail us, and we will fail them. God alone remains faithful, loving and perfect. God alone will not fail us.

Communities and their leaders eventually show their dysfunctions and sinful ways of relating. Your parish priest, the director of your RCIA formation, the nun who runs the community meal, the president of the Catholic Women's League, the recruiter for the Knights of Columbus, the principal of the Catholic school to which you were so excited to send your children, and the wonderful friends you have made during your preparation – all these will also, in small and sometimes large ways, display pettiness, greed, dishonesty, unkindness or any other number of sinful characteristics.

This will happen in a community despite our best intentions. I'll give you a personal example. As background, you need to know that I pride myself on my peacemaking skills. When I was a young girl, I was the one on the playground trying to reconcile warring factions. This continued throughout high school and university and well into my professional life. I generally have an ability to see the good in mostly everyone, so I'm not often the one "at war." That is the context.

Here is the story. A few years ago, a woman I had been preparing for initiation stopped coming to our meetings. I waited a few weeks and puzzled about what might have caused her to stop attending. I had witnessed a slight tension between her and another team member, so I figured he must have offended her. I called her after she missed the third session. I asked her if everything was okay.

"No," she replied curtly. Silence.

"Did someone offend you?" I queried.

"As a matter of fact, they did," she admitted. I *knew* it. That man!

"Was it Joe?" I offered, sure that I had figured out the problem. (Names, of course, have been changed to protect the innocent who, in this case, are truly innocent.)

"No, it wasn't Joe. Quite honestly," she said and, after a pause, continued, "it was… it was you."

> Faith has to be inside yourself. If people are not very kind or the church is awful, at the end of the day, these are "people" things. Going to church is not about all of these things. It is about meeting God.
> —Aylin öztürk Akşen

Then she explained what I had done that had deeply hurt her, including waiting two weeks before calling to see why she wasn't attending our gatherings. I was flabbergasted. I had not intended to hurt, but it was clear that I had... and deeply. I apologized sincerely, but the woman never did return. I am not sure what happened to her after this incident. I hope she found a place where she could practise her faith if she wasn't able to find it at our parish because of my insensitivity. But I don't know. It was a humbling but significant moment in my life. I learned that none of us can place our faith in a person. Sometimes not even in oneself.

We ought to hold our brothers and sisters in Christ, especially our religious leaders, to high standards of honesty, integrity and morality. However, they *will* fail us, and we *will* fail them. God alone remains faithful, loving and perfect. God alone will not fail us.

Finally, the Church itself will likely disappoint you at some point. Catholics believe the Holy Spirit provides divine guidance to the Church. Jesus promised that the Spirit would lead us and inspire us from the time of Christ's Ascension into heaven until his final return. However, guidance and inspiration do not mean that God forces us to be good. We often are not. One does not need to delve deeply into history books to see that this holy Church of Jesus Christ has been, in serious ways, much less than holy. From the persecution of non-believers to the treatment of Indigenous peoples to the sexual abuse of children, people in the Church – sometimes even in the name of the Church – have perpetrated great evil and injustice. This cannot be denied if we are honest about who we are. We are a pilgrim Church. That is, we are on our way to becoming what Christ calls us to be. We are not there yet. So, expect that even the Church will fail us, and we will fail it. God alone remains faithful, loving and perfect. God alone will not fail us.

Idol Worship – Don't Settle for a Small God

It is not enough, however, to place God at the centre of our faith. In making God the centre, we must also avoid idol worship. Yes, that's right – idol worship. This may seem an odd thing to warn someone about in the 21st century. The image that often comes to mind when we hear the term "idol worship" is that of the Israelites in the desert worshipping a golden calf. Such idolatry is not much of a temptation in modern times. However, there are contemporary forms of idolatry in which we worship as God something that is less than God – wealth, status, success and a myriad of other things. Sometimes, even the idea of God can also be the subject of idol-like devotion.

The God we place at the centre of our faith has to be God. The true God is more than we can ever conceive or imagine. The true God is, and will always remain, a mystery. Even if we were to devote every moment of our lives to searching for God, God would remain a mystery – a "knowable" mystery, but a mystery nonetheless. Our images of God will (and ought to) expand and deepen over our lifetime. This is why in Scripture a great variety of images are used to describe God: mother, father, lover, rock, creator, friend, saviour, Lord. By some counts, Scripture contains nearly a thousand different images of God. Add images used by the saints through the ages, and there are even more.

The God who Christ proclaims to us is not simply a God who makes us feel good, but a God who challenges us to move out of our comfort zones. To use a popular phrase, God "comforts the afflicted and afflicts the comfortable." God cannot be defined but constantly reveals Godself to us. God can give us strength to bear our burdens and can inspire us to accomplish feats of love and beauty beyond our wildest imagination.

A God Big Enough to Support Challenge

At the centre of our faith and worship, we must place what I like to think of as a "big enough" God. We will know that the God in whom we believe is a big enough God because this God can withstand the challenges of questioning and doubt. We need not be afraid of questions that we can't answer because when God is this great, "I don't know" is a reasonable response. You can say, "I don't know this, that or the other thing about the mystery of God, but that is okay, because I have had an encounter with God and experienced a Divine Presence that I know to be true. I have experienced something that empowers me. I have met someone I believe in. I don't have all the answers, and quite frankly I never will, but still I believe." This is faith.

Theologian Paul Tillich taught that the opposite of faith is not doubt. The opposite of faith is certainty. Faith in a God of mystery can withstand doubt. The Church even has a patron saint of doubters – his name is Thomas. He stood before the Risen Christ and declared, "Unless I see the mark of the nails in his hands and put my finger in the mark of the nails and my hand in his side, I will not believe." (John 20:25) Jesus indulged Thomas, letting him place his hand in the wound in his side. Then he declared, "Blessed are those who have not seen and yet have come to believe." Thomas was imperfect in faith, but still the Church celebrates him as a saint. So don't be concerned that your concept of God is not crystal clear. In fact, be concerned if it is.

The Church teaches that each of us constantly experiences God's presence and self-communication. We are not always aware of it, but it is always our reality. Sometimes when we share our experiences of God with one another, we can seem to come into conflict. One person's experience of God may not only be different from ours, but may contradict it. Many times, this conversation comes up early in our catechetical sessions as we prepare people for initiation. I often use an African folk tale of which there are many versions. The short version is that there is a village of blind folks. Being blind, the villagers have hearing that is heightened. One day they hear a distant sound that they do not understand. A scout is sent to discover the source of the sound and determine if it is a threat. A few days later, the scout returns and says the sound is coming from an animal that is extremely large and soft which could smother the inhabitants of the village.

Aware of their blindness, the villagers send a second scout for confirmation. This scout returns with the message that the first scout was wrong. This animal bears two sword-like weapons which could impale villagers. More confused than ever, the villagers send out a third scout, who returns saying the beast was snake-like and could strangle them. It turned out that all the scouts met the same animal. It was an elephant. But because they were blind and because they encountered only a small part of the massive animal, their descriptions appeared to be contradictory. They were, in fact, not contradictory but partial – a belly, a tusk and a trunk. It is like this with our image of God. We all have partial, blind but true encounters.

God is ultimately a mystery. It is also true, however, that God is knowable. God is majestic, and yet also intimately and warmly present to us as a daddy. God is Father; God is Mother. These images are not contradictory. They are necessary to help us understand a God who is big enough to believe in.

So, if you find yourself in a discussion with someone who disputes your understanding of God, bear them with patience. You are both in the presence of God. You are simply encountering a different aspect of this mystery depending upon your honest but blind encounter with a Divinity too great to be summed up in one person's conception.

A God Big Enough to Bear Our Burdens

As a child I spent a lot of time at my great-grandmother's house. A religious picture of some sort hung on every wall, in every room. Most of them were large, even imposing.

When you entered the house, it was clear that faith played a central role there. Today's real estate agents would insist on restaging this house immediately. Way too personal! Way too religious! Who would buy a house where the Sacred Heart of Jesus dominates in such a way?

The place that religious images had in my great-grandmother's house reflected the God she believed in. Grandma believed in a big God. A second-generation Irish immigrant, she was a farmer's wife in a difficult marriage at a time when people stayed in difficult marriages no matter how tough they were. She worked hard from morning till evening and had to make do with little to ensure a basic level of comfort. Despite all this, I cannot recall ever hearing my grandmother complain. She had a strength that I now regard as courageous. She also had faith in a God who was big enough and strong enough to get her through her trials. The larger-than-life pictures on her wall were a visual signal of that God. The God of my great-grandmother was a God upon whom she could place her substantial burdens; it was a big enough God to sustain her.

This same "God Beyond All Praising"[1] is the God whom suffering humanity has relied upon throughout the ages. No one escapes life without suffering. For some people, that suffering is almost unbearable. Perhaps you yourself have been through this kind of suffering. Many of those with whom I have worked have come to church precisely because they need help understanding and bearing their suffering. The God we believe in must be big enough to help us bear our burdens.

You can find images of this kind of God not only in the artwork of my great-grandmother's wall, but also in the songs and poetry of persecuted Christians. From the cries of Job, who in his suffering acclaimed, "Blessed be God," to the songs of the Christian slaves who sang, "There is a balm in Gilead to make the wounded whole," believers have relied on God to strengthen them and give them courage.

Finally, a truly great God has inspired people to tremendous acts of love and sacrifice and to monumental acts of beauty. For this One, True God, people have been willing to give their lives in the service of others. Sometimes they speak up in the face of injustice and die a martyr's death – as Archbishop Romero of El Salvador did. Sometimes they give their lives in service – as Mother Teresa of Kolkata did. For this Living Mystery, the great cathedrals of the world have been built. For this Awesome Creator, some of the most beautiful music in the world has been written. Such accomplishments witness to faith in a God worthy of spending one's entire life for.

So, before all else, if you want this faith of yours to last you a lifetime, make sure it is faith in a God in whom you can proclaim, "How great Thou art! How great Thou art!"[2]

PRACTICAL SUGGESTIONS

Look up images of God in Scripture and use
each image in prayer for a week.

Find an image of God that makes you uncomfortable and
pray using that image. Often the images that make us
most uncomfortable are the ones that can help expose
our "idolatries" and can help us to grow
in understanding.

Read the writings of saints and martyrs and
explore their favourite images of God.

Listen to some African American spirituals.
The experience can be enriched by learning the
history and developing an understanding of how
these songs provided solace and strength to people
in times of suffering.

Read the Book of Job in the Bible.

If you can, visit the great churches of Europe. If you can't
visit in person, watch a video or do an online tour.

Experience the "awesomeness of God" in creation.
Spend time in the natural world, especially in places
like the Grand Canyon or Niagara Falls or the Rocky
Mountains, where awe is the only appropriate response.

Talk to other people about how they imagine
and experience God.

Visit a beautiful place of worship.

2

FOSTER A SOLID PERSONAL PRAYER LIFE

The Centrality of Prayer

The practice of prayer was central in the life of every saint throughout history. It can be difficult to make time for prayer, but prayer is necessary to keep God at the core of our lives and to sustain our faith. St. Francis de Sales is reputed to have said that every Christian needs a half hour of prayer each day, except when they're busy: then the person needs an hour. Faith in the Living God is fundamentally a relationship of love. This relationship can only be sustained if we spend time with our Beloved. The love we have for God can be quite similar to a human love relationship. It begins with a high level of intensity and then, as it matures, settles into something much more ordinary, comfortable and habitual, but nonetheless beautiful. The ordinariness of a mature relationship with God is not a bad thing. My husband and I have coffee together every morning. He likes to read the paper; I like to sit and stare into space. Typically, few words, if any, are exchanged between us. We are just "being together." It is a habit, it is not particularly inspiring, but it is an essential part of sustaining our relationship. So it is with our relationship with God. Prayer is a non-negotiable.

Types of Prayer

While prayer is a non-negotiable, the options for prayer are as varied as the people who pray. The Church offers us a wealth of prayer forms. You may have already been introduced to some of them, but more remain to be discovered. More on that later. For now, however, it is important to develop a prayer life that is balanced and healthy.

The Christian tradition has four main types of prayer. We know them as intercessory prayer (praying for someone), prayers of petition (praying for something), prayers of thanksgiving and prayers of praise. One author concisely sums this up as "Help! Thanks! Wow!"[3] For prayer to be balanced, it should not resemble a Christmas wish list. "Dear God, please give me this, that and the other thing." However noble and good our requests of God are (health, happiness, the good of others), if all we do when we pray is ask for things, we are not in a relationship of love. We must also pray in gratitude and praise. A fifth type of prayer important in a mature spiritual life is the prayer of contemplation. Contemplation is simply putting ourselves in the presence of God, being open and listening, but primarily just "being." It is very much like the quiet time my husband and I spend in the mornings together.

A few more elements are important for a healthy and balanced prayer life. You will need to spend time alone with God, and you will need to spend time praying with others. You will want to memorize some of the prayers of the Catholic tradition, and you will want to learn how to pray spontaneously from the depths of your heart. Let us now look further into each of these aspects.

Prayer Alone and Prayer in Community

Personal prayer and communal prayer are both important for Catholics. Each contributes to the health of the other. In our personal prayer, alone with our God, we become closer to God. We are given insights which we can contribute to the great Christian community. In communal prayer, we become closer to God as well as to our brothers and sisters in faith, and we are given insights that we could not arrive at on our own. Engaging in both personal and communal prayer helps to keep us honest. Many times, people say, "I don't need to go to church; I can pray to God anywhere." While it is true that you can pray anywhere and everywhere, and indeed, Jesus tells us to "pray always" (Luke 18:1), private prayer is not enough. Without the "testing ground" of the community, we are easily deluded into hearing only messages of solace that do not challenge us to grow beyond our comfort zone. The voice of God, spoken from outside us, is critical to testing that the voice we hear in prayer is genuinely the voice of God rather than a voice that tells us what we want to hear. Likewise, communities of faith can fall into a similar trap. That is why we need to retreat, as Jesus did in the desert, to be alone with our God and bring the wisdom that we gain in private prayer to our community.

The primary communal prayer in which we engage as Roman Catholics is Sunday Mass, but Catholics also engage in other forms of communal prayer, such as prayer groups and pilgrimages. Catholics gather together to pray the Way of the Cross, to say the rosary and to pray before the Blessed Sacrament. More will be said about these prayer forms later in this chapter.

Written Prayer and Spontaneous Prayer

Two types of prayer that you will also want to have in your prayer "toolbox" are the well-known formal prayers of the Church, which you have memorized, as well as spontaneous prayer – speaking to God from the heart. The latter is the most natural way for most people to pray. We just bring our thoughts, worries, fears, hopes and joys to God as we would bring such things to a conversation with a friend. Spontaneous prayer is typically the form of prayer we use when we are alone with God. Catholics do not have a strong tradition of spontaneous prayer in groups. Most of the time when Catholics gather, we find comfort in either a memorized prayer or prayers that have been written out. Spontaneous communal prayer does exist in Catholicism, however, especially within charismatic prayer groups. If this is the kind of communal prayer that suits you, and it might be, especially if you have come from an Evangelical Protestant tradition, it is well worth seeking out a group that prays in this fashion.

More typical of communal prayer for Catholics is the use of memorized or written-out prayers. These are appealing for a number of reasons. They are wonderful when we are in situations where words fail us. I have always loved the tradition of saying the rosary at the wake (visitation) service when someone dies. What can really be said at such a time, after all? All our words are inadequate. So, we admit that we have no perfect words to take away the sadness of those who are left behind. Instead, we join together to pray repetitions of the Our Father, Hail Mary and Glory Be. Memorized prayers and prayers that have been written by others and put into books are also helpful when you gather as a group and wish to begin with prayer. Anyone can begin a meeting with the Lord's Prayer (and what could be better than the prayer that Jesus himself taught?). Finally, many well-known prayers of the Church are beautiful. Few of us are capable of writing poetry as wonderful as the Prayer of St. Francis or the *Suscipe* of St. Ignatius. (These are prayers you might want to research as part of your ongoing learning as a new Catholic.) These well-known prayers, as well as prayers written by those who are gifted wordsmiths, can help us say things to God we didn't even know we wanted to say. Finally, such written prayers can be a way of bringing others into our private prayer to help us expand our understanding of God's communication to us.

Once we ensure that our prayer is balanced in these ways, we need to find forms of prayers that work best for our individual personality types and temperaments. When my husband and I were studying for our theology degrees, we took a course together that turned out to be the best thing we ever did for our relationship with each other and the best thing we ever did for our relationships with God. The course was called *Life of Prayer*. The professor began by making us take the Myers-Briggs personality type indicator test. He told us that if we understand who we are as individuals, how we take in and process information, how we communicate and relate to others, and how we learn, we will be much more likely to find a prayer form that works for us. Prayer is about communication. Knowing how we communicate is essential to developing a healthy relationship with God. (Incidentally, it is also important to developing a healthy relationship with one's spouse – which is why this course was also one of the best things we did for our relationship.)

After establishing our personality attributes, the class spent the rest of the weeks experimenting with forms of prayer. As the professor predicted, some worked marvellously well and others not so much. What worked depended, not surprisingly, upon our communication style. We can be grateful that the Catholic tradition provides as many different prayer forms as there are personality types – perhaps even more. If we are serious about our spiritual life, we must pray often. After this, the options are abundant.

PRACTICAL SUGGESTIONS

Connect with God in an intentional way every day – morning and night at the very least.

Memorize the important prayers of the Church. You'll typically find these in the "Traditional Prayers" section of any prayer book. They include the Lord's Prayer, Hail Mary and Glory Be. Several others would enrich your faith life: the Prayer of St. Francis, the Memorare, and the Acts of Faith, Hope and Charity.

Purchase a couple of good prayer books. Sometimes other people can articulate thoughts, hopes and dreams that you didn't realize you had.

Set up a prayer space in your home. This can be a chair with a small table on which you keep a Bible, an icon, a rosary or anything else that helps you enter into prayer.

Attend any and all prayer services that your parish and neighbouring parishes offer so you can experience a variety of prayer forms. You will not love them all, but you will be surprised at how many of them help you encounter God more profoundly.

When considering praying in groups, think about including ecumenical (with people from varied Christian traditions) and interfaith (with people of non-Christian faith) prayer experiences.

CATHOLIC PRAYER –
A WEALTH OF POSSIBILITIES

As you explore the wide variety of prayer forms the Church offers, you will find that many can be done either alone or with others. As you continue to grow in your knowledge and practice of the faith, try everything you find appealing… and maybe even some that you don't. You may be surprised to find what works for you. In the next few pages, you will find a description of some favourite forms of Catholic prayer.

Praying with Sacred Scripture & Lectio Divina – God speaks to us in the Sacred Scriptures, so praying with Scripture in some fashion should play a central role in our prayer life. We can do this in a number of ways:

> Read the readings of the day. Use a printed missalette or a smartphone app. *Living with Christ*, published by Novalis, is available in both paper and digital versions and features the text used in the Lectionary (the book of readings used at Mass) in Canada. Find a resource that provides reflections on the readings. Ask for guidance from your pastoral leaders so you are directed to the best versions.

> Work slowly through a book of the Bible, reading only a small bit each day and then reflecting on what the passage says to you. The Gospels or the Psalms are good places to start. A Scripture commentary can provide you with background information on the Scripture you are reading, though you can certainly pray with the Bible without a commentary.

> Learn about the tradition of *Lectio Divina*. This is an ancient way of praying with Scripture slowly and intentionally.

Liturgy of the Hours or the Divine Office – The Divine Office is the official prayer book of the Church. This ancient prayer is required by all those who are ordained or vowed to religious life. It has, in more recent times, also become popular with lay Catholics. You may hear it referred to as the Breviary, the Divine Office or the Liturgy of the Hours. It consists of acclamations, psalms and readings from the writings of the saints. Specific prayers are assigned for each time of the day: morning, noon, evening and night. The tradition of praying at specific hours throughout the day "is devised so that the whole course of the day and night is made holy by the praises of God."[4] Historically, some prayers were developed for early in the morning, and others for late at night. Unless you suffer from insomnia or join a monastery, you are not likely to use these prayers. But you may want to learn about *Lauds* (Morning Prayer) and *Vespers* (Evening Prayer).

The Divine Office can be prayed either alone or with others. In some parishes, people regularly pray Morning or Evening Prayer together. As with the rosary, the Office probably needs to be learned in a group before it can be effective as private prayer.

> Look for a parish that offers the Liturgy of the Hours (usually either Morning Prayer or Evening Prayer).

> Find online versions or phone apps of the Divine Office.

Stations of the Cross – The Stations of the Cross (or Way of the Cross) is a traditional Catholic prayer form that has existed since around the 15th century. It is an expression of the deeply rooted desire people have to touch the things a person they admire touched and to see what they saw. This desire is why tours of Hollywood are so popular. Not surprisingly, this was also the case for Christians of ancient times, as it is for us today. Christians sought to visit the places of Christ's life, particularly where he was crucified. As the Holy Land became a place of great danger and as Christianity spread geographically further away from Israel, this became impossible for most people. In the 1500s, the Franciscans (the community of men founded by St. Francis of Assisi) began to build a series of "stations" depicting scenes from Jesus' passion. Christians could walk from scene to scene, imagining what it would have been like to be present at the time of Christ. Today, you will find Stations of the Cross gracing the walls of almost every Catholic church in the world. If we wish to walk in Christ's footsteps, we need only visit our local parish.

The Stations can be prayed alone or with others. Groups of Catholics often get together to pray the Way of the Cross during Lent, though it can be prayed any time of the year. Typically, the prayer involves meditating on a specific moment of Christ's passion and then reflecting on how it relates to us in our own lives.

> Purchase a Way of the Cross book. Try some of the countless versions until you find a few that speak to you.
> Attend the Stations of the Cross at your church.
> Visit an outdoor Stations of the Cross. These are common at shrines and pilgrimage sites. (I once stumbled on one that was in a roadside park. While we didn't have time to do a full version of the prayer, our family walked past all the stops and was grateful for the reminder to pause and pray.)

> Pray the Stations alone, either in the church or at home.
> This prayer form has inspired countless artists, and many inspirational versions of the Stations have been created. Pinterest is a wonderful source for artistic interpretations of the Way of the Cross. Look online for the art of this devotion and use it for your prayer even without the text.

The Rosary – The rosary is probably the prayer that most people associate with Catholicism. The rosary is a way of using prayer beads to help focus and enter into a state of meditation. Prayer beads do not belong to Catholics alone; you will also find them used in the Anglican tradition as well as in non-Christian religions. Buddhists, Hindus and Muslims all use prayer beads. While praying with beads or knotted rope is an ancient tradition, the rosary more or less as we know it today became popularized by St. Dominic in the 13th century.

The rosary is a series of repeated prayers: Our Father, Hail Mary and Glory Be. It begins with the Apostles' Creed and can include other prayers as well. A full rosary consists of five decades (sets of one Our Father and ten Hail Marys). The word "decade" comes from the Latin word meaning ten. Sometimes people pray just one decade. This is one Our Father, ten Hail Marys and one Glory Be. Other times, people will pray five decades. This amounts to one circle around the rosary beads.

Sometimes when people who are unfamiliar with the rosary hear it, they feel people are racing through prayers with little intentionality. The repeated prayers, however, are not so much to be the focus of our reflection – though they can be, if you like – but rather serve as a mantra to calm our mind into a meditative state so we can reflect on the mysteries of Christ's life. The rosary has four different types of mystery. These lead us through the stages of Jesus' life. The joyful mysteries deal with his early life, the luminous mysteries with his teaching ministry, the sorrowful mysteries with his crucifixion and death, and the glorious mysteries with his resurrection and its meaning for us as his disciples.

As a small child, I prayed the rosary with my great-grandmother before bed each night. I thought the whole point was to get through it as fast as possible. I would engage in the un-prayerful exercise of trying to get my part of the prayers said as fast as I could without leaving out any words. I could have been helped by a proper explanation of why we repeated those words over and over.

As with the Stations of the Cross, the rosary can be prayed alone or with others. Many people find that it is easiest to learn when prayed with groups. Until the structure of the prayer is learned, its mantra-like function doesn't occur. So, to give the rosary a fair chance as prayer, it is best to spend time learning it well.

> Buy a rosary and attend a rosary group at your church.
> Download an audible rosary app to your phone and pray along with it.
> Pray the rosary as you drive. Mind you, it is best to do this with a recording or once you've learned the prayer well. You *do* still need to concentrate on your driving no matter how religious you are.
> Attend a living rosary where each participant represents a bead of the rosary.
> Learn about other lesser-known prayer bead traditions such as the Chaplet of Divine Mercy.

> Make your own rosary. This can be a prayerful and meditative experience itself. Supplies are easily obtained online or at any jewellery-making supplier.

Praying with Music and Art – Catholics believe in using all our senses in prayer. Thus, praying with our eyes and ears can help us communicate more effectively with God as well as with our friends and family. Music and art can touch us at an emotional level that can have a powerful and lasting effect on us spiritually and can convey our deepest emotions and thoughts. The emotional impact of music explains why couples spend a lot of time deciding on the song they will play for the first dance at their wedding, or why we strongly associate people and events with particular songs. Songs can also stick with us as reminders of God's presence. If you are like me and are susceptible to earworms (those songs that get stuck in your head for hours), why not have it be "Be Not Afraid"[5] rather than "I Want to Be a Billionaire So Freakin' Bad"? I am always delighted when I hear my teenage children (who absolutely refuse to open their mouths in church no matter how much they have been encouraged to do so) singing Mass parts to themselves while walking around the house on a Sunday afternoon. St. Augustine taught that "The one who sings prays twice." He didn't say anything about how much we are praying if we hum the same refrain over and over throughout the day, but I'm sure it counts for something. Music can be a vehicle for helping us to pray constantly and for bringing just the right phrase to mind when we need it.

Religious art can have the same function. Beauty is an attribute of divinity. Gazing intently at a piece of art or praying before an icon can sometimes lead us to insight that words may never be able to do. This is sometimes referred to as *Visio Divina* – sacred seeing (to parallel *Lectio Divina* – sacred reading). Surrounding ourselves with religious art can be a continual reminder of our good God's constant presence.

You may even use your own drawing or painting as a way to express your religious feelings and thoughts. Meditative "adult" colouring is currently popular, but it is actually an ancient tradition. In Buddhism, the creation of mandalas is a way to use repetitive pattern-making as a mantra to quiet and centre the mind. In Islam, artists intentionally embed errors in their art to remind themselves that only God is perfect. These traditions correspond beautifully with Catholicism.

Finally, both art and music can be effective ways to place us in a state of quiet so we can enter more deeply into the presence of God through meditation.

> ‣ Place religious images in your home. Icons are an especially powerful form of religious art and are regarded by Eastern Christians with the same level of reverence as Western Christians regard the Eucharist. Gazing upon an icon can be parallel to praying before the Blessed Sacrament (Eucharistic devotion).

> ‣ Explore the art of faith. Do not limit yourself to common European art. Explore religious art from Asia, Africa, the Americas. A number of blogs offer meditations on religious art, often in conjunction with the Sunday Lectionary readings.

> ‣ Place a crucifix in your home. Some Catholics place a crucifix above the doorways. Think about using one that reflects your particular culture. In our home, we have

a St. Brigid's cross in one room, a Ukrainian cross in another, and Salvadoran, Indigenous and Celtic crosses in others. (We have many ethnic groups represented in our family... and also a fair number of doorways in our home.)

> Place an image of the Last Supper in your dining room.
> Purchase a colouring book of Scripture verse illustrations. Many of these adult colouring pages are available free online.
> Try the practice of Bible journalling and Bible "doodle art."
> Paint, draw or doodle your prayers.
> Sing (even if people are listening).
> Listen to religious music first thing in the morning.
> Download some of your favourite hymns onto your music player.
> Learn the history of some of the songs we sing in church. Knowing their origins and associated stories can enrich the manner in which the song leads you to insight and prayer.
> Explore Taizé prayer in a church or retreat centre that offers it. Taizé is an ecumenical community in France known for its style of repetitive and meditative chant which has become known worldwide. You may have been introduced to it on Holy Thursday if your parish uses the chant "Ubi Caritas."

Retreats and Pilgrimages – Sometimes to have a different perspective, we need to *literally* get a different perspective. That is, we need to look at our lives from a new vantage point. Retreats and pilgrimages are ways in which the Church helps us do this. We take time away from busy lives, cellphones, to-do lists – even people – to focus on God. When we go on retreats and pilgrimages, we can return emotionally, spiritually and even physically refreshed, having looked at our life from a different space.

Retreats are like a time-out in which we free ourselves from distractions to focus only on prayer. Retreats can be for an evening, a day, a weekend or even longer. Jesuit retreat houses offer thirty-day silent retreats. That is a serious time-out. As a new Catholic, you may need to work up to that level. Retreats can be led by a director or self-directed.

Pilgrimages are trips to a sacred destination. This form of religious practice is found in almost every great religious tradition and is even a requirement for some (such as in Islam). In a pilgrimage, we physically move our bodies to a sacred site as a sign of our desire to move our spirits closer to God. The physical journey symbolizes our spiritual journey. People make pilgrimages to the Holy Land, to sites of apparitions and to beautiful churches.

Visiting beautiful churches is another way to engage in *Visio Divina*. Standing in the presence of great architecture can help one develop a sense of God's greatness, as well as connect one's burgeoning faith with the impressive faith of those people who spent their lives (sometimes the lives of multiple generations) creating these great edifices that testify to faith. We can learn about the Christian story by seeing it depicted on the walls of the churches. We can be drawn to place ourselves in that story in new ways. Each form of architecture can lead us to a different kind of prayer. Great Gothic cathedrals can help us pray prayers of praise. Richly decorated Baroque churches can help us pray in gratitude for beauty and blessings. Oratory walls covered in the no-longer-needed crutches of those who have been cured of illness can help us pray in intercession for our own healing. Small, simple country churches can create a sense in us of God's nearness and love for us. The possibilities for insight and inspiration are limited only to our openness to receive them.

Pilgrimages are a wonderful way not only to become closer to God but also to become closer to other members of the Church. Nothing builds community like sitting in the back of the bus singing "This Little Light of Mine."

> I learned about a pilgrimage in Spain called "the way," or in Spanish, *El Camino*. It is a pilgrimage where you hike 800 km with a backpack to the resting place of St. James (one of the twelve Apostles of Christ) in Santiago de Compostela. So, after getting all the approvals and lots of training, I went in 2015 and learned so much. I started to pray the rosary every day and stopped at every church along the way to say thanks and pray for greater faith and for people. I thought I would be lonely, but I met so many people and enjoyed the conversations and the company. I remember thinking the biggest weight we carry in life is fear. There is a saying along El Camino, "The Camino will provide," and it sure did. I always found shelter, food and never felt alone. God provided. I felt a presence inside of me and around me and in others. It helped me to feel others' pain and suffering, to care about all people.—Gary Marston

Finally, pilgrimages do not all have to end at explicitly religious places. You can develop a deep awareness of the presence of God by visiting "God's own cathedrals." The natural wonders of the world can be a place where the Creator communicates to us through creation. One year, our family visited the Grand Canyon. We drove there. More accurately, we drove and drove and drove and *drove* there! (We live in the Toronto area.) By the time we arrived, we had developed a sense of how large this continent is and, by extrapolation, how large the planet is. If the distance we drove didn't make us aware of how small we are in this universe, standing on the precipice of the Grand Canyon certainly did. On this same vacation, we also visited Petrified Forest National Park where we saw trees that existed 250 million years ago. A human person takes up at most one square foot of space standing up and, if we're lucky, around ninety years of time. By experiencing space and time the way we did on this trip, it became apparent that we are but grains of sand and blips of time in the universe. It was humbling. Yet, at the same time, in these places of majesty I had a sense that despite my smallness, I was deeply valued by a loving God and that, in some way, all this beauty before me was a gift just for me. Awareness of that gift led me to a sense of the grandeur and beauty of the One who had created it.

Encounters with nature and knowledge of the natural world can be places where the Creator is revealed through creation. The medieval mystic Julian of Norwich once meditated on a hazelnut.[6] She noticed the beauty of the wood of the shell that protected the hazelnut until it was time for it to become the seed of a new tree. Such reflection gave her insight into God's love for creation. We might do the same, asking, "If God could take such care to create an exquisite, intricately grained shell for a mere hazelnut, how much more does God care for us?"

It is no accident that Jesus used metaphors from the natural world to teach us about God. So, if you want to know more about God, take time to "consider the lilies." (Matthew 6:28) It is no mistake that the sacraments of the Church use the gifts of nature to communicate the realities of God's life and goodness: water, oil, fire, beeswax, light, darkness, dirt, flowers, human touch and more. This faith which you have chosen can be experienced in all things. The world is a sacrament to you of God's love. In the words of poet Gerard Manley Hopkins, "The world is charged with the Grandeur of God."[7] Pray it and your prayer will take place with a constancy that you can only begin to imagine.

Sometimes retreats and pilgrimage are combined. Both can be done alone or with others, though most pilgrimages are done as a group.

> Look up retreats and pilgrimages offered in your local area and find one that interests you.
> Do an online retreat. The Irish Jesuits have a wonderful prayer site called Sacred Space where they offer a daily three-minute retreat (www.sacredspace.ie).
> If you have the financial means and the physical ability, walk the Camino of St. James (Santiago) in Spain. If you don't, walk to church some Sunday.
> Walk a labyrinth. This is an ancient form of prayer that is like a mini-pilgrimage in which a person walks the path of a maze-like pattern on the ground. Unlike a maze, however, there are no dead ends. Everyone arrives at the centre. This reminds us that we are all ultimately on a journey to closer union with God, the centre of our lives. You can find labyrinths on the floors of churches and even in parks. In Toronto, one labyrinth is located near

the Eaton Centre in Trinity Square. There are labyrinth colouring pages and miniature labyrinths you can trace with your finger. All of them can help us centre and focus on our slow and steady journey inward to God.

> Read books about science and reflect on how the Creator communicates through creation.
> Reflect on the Scripture passages in which Jesus uses the natural world to teach about God.
> Use natural objects as a focus for prayer. Light candles when you pray. Use holy water and holy oil and incense.

Meditative and Contemplative Prayer – A variety of forms of meditative or contemplative prayer are popular with Catholics.

The *Examen* is a prayer that comes from St. Ignatius of Loyola. He encouraged people to take time at the end of the day to reflect on God's action in their lives. In this prayer, you look back upon your day and think about times in which you have experienced God's presence and God's absence. You consider the blessings for which you can give thanks, the struggles for which you can ask for assistance and the actions for which you need forgiveness. The prayer ends by asking God to help you be more attentive to God's presence and making a commitment to live more lovingly and justly on the following day. Many people find it helpful to combine the *Examen* with journalling.

Journalling can be an effective way to help formulate your conversation with God. Writing letters to God about your hopes and dreams, your struggles and successes can sometimes help focus your attention in prayer and keep your mind from wandering. Indeed, many saints kept journals which now hold a place among the classics of Christian literature.

If you are going to journal, you may want to invest in an attractive book explicitly for that purpose. Catholics have a deep appreciation of beauty. Indeed, as noted earlier, we see it as an attribute of the Divine. This is why we use beautiful items for sacred purposes. Think of chalices, Lectionaries, vestments. If you want to make grocery lists, by all means use the notepad that came in the mail with the latest fund-raising appeal. But if you want to pray, use something worthy of prayer.

Eucharistic Devotion is another popular Catholic contemplative prayer in which people sit before the Blessed Sacrament and reflect on Christ's gift of Presence. It can be done either alone or with others. When done with others, there are specific prayers and songs which are typically used.

› Pray the Examen.
› Pray with a mantra. A mantra is a phrase that is repeated over and over. The most common is the Jesus Prayer: "Lord Jesus Christ, Son of God, have mercy on me, a sinner."
› Begin a prayer journal.
› Attend communal Benediction and Eucharistic Adoration in a parish where it is offered.
› Sit in quiet contemplation before the Blessed Sacrament.

As you continue to live your life as a Catholic, experiment with the great variety of prayer forms that the Church offers. Try everything that appeals to you and some things that don't. You never know what you might discover.

3

LIVE LITURGICALLY

The Source and Summit of Christian Life

The ultimate prayer, for all Catholics, is the Sunday celebration of the Eucharist. The Church teaches that it is the source and summit of our life of faith.[8] That is, the Eucharist is where we go for sustenance – where we drink from the well of God's refreshing love, where we are fed on the Real Presence of Christ. It is also the place where we go "up to the mountain of God" to obtain a clearer vision of our lives and our place in creation. Joining the Church without committing to Sunday Eucharist is like joining a hockey team with no intention of playing the game. Catholics go to Mass. It's part of the definition of who we are.

If you are serious about keeping this newly professed faith of yours alive, you need to attend Sunday Mass. Every Sunday. Every *single* Sunday. Making a priority of worshipping every Sunday reminds us that God, and God alone, is the centre of our life. Not work. Not sports. Not sleeping in. God.

The presence of the Lord is real in the Eucharist and in the life of the Church. As we grow in grace, the Lord becomes more real and present to us.—Joanne Barnett

Going to Mass helped me become a member of a community and develop a feeling of belonging. Going to Mass opened my heart to Jesus and helped me to understand what he did for us and a path of life we need to take.—Gary Marston

Frequent the sacraments. Read the Catechism. Attempt to get involved in parish life, but don't get disheartened or discouraged if various forms of involvement are less than successful for you personally. The Eucharist is the summit of our faith; even very good things such as fellowship do not displace the Eucharist in importance.—Cecilia Beale

Many cradle Catholics grew up with the fear that if we missed Mass on Sunday, we had better put on our flame-retardant underwear in case we got hit by a bus before we managed to get to Confession. In some ways (minus the fear factor), the Church did us a favour by forcefully demanding weekly church attendance. It removed our burden of choice. We knew we had to go. Weekly Mass attendance was a non-negotiable. We are still expected to attend Mass weekly. However, in the culture in which most of us live today, the burden of choosing to attend rests solely on us. We do not have a larger community watching us and ensuring that we are in church on Sunday morning. Missing Mass involves no social stigma. It is up to us to place weekly Eucharist at the centre of our commitment, with or without the support of the surrounding community.

It's not a big deal to miss Mass occasionally, is it? Giving yourself permission to miss the occasional Mass becomes a slippery slope and, before you know it, you haven't been to church in weeks. Ask many "lapsed" Catholics, and you'll hear that this is a familiar tale. You may not immediately feel the loss. The parish community may not immediately feel the loss. But there *is* a loss. The body is broken; it is not whole. We need everyone here. We need *you* here. If even one person is missing from the table, the banquet is not the celebration it is meant to be.

Not every Mass you attend will necessarily *feel* like a summit moment. Nevertheless, every Mass nourishes us as Christians. Think of how meals nourish us. Not all of them are memorable. Occasionally a meal is so delicious that we think about it for days or even remember it for years. But most meals, even when we are fed with tasty, nutritious food, fade in our consciousness. Nevertheless, every single one is vital for our ongoing physical sustenance. We need them all – the oatmeal breakfasts and the turkey dinners with all the fixings. Our physical feeding and our spiritual feeding run parallel. On occasion, we will leave Sunday Mass with a deep sense of satisfaction: the music, the homily and the reception of the Eucharist will have taken us to a place of "transfiguration." But the celebration of the Mass does not always take us to such an emotional place. Sometimes you will feel no enthusiasm about the worship experience or may even be bored. We are not always in the right psychological space to recognize the great gift given by God. As a Christian community, we do not always do the best job of communicating that great gift to one another. However, even without our awareness, the celebration of the Eucharist always contributes to our spiritual nourishment and remains crucial to the vitality of our Christian faith.

> I need it... It's just an hour once a week, but it gives me peace. It's a time-out for me... to think, to relax, to just focus on one thing.—Laurie O'Heir

A Home Anywhere in the World

One wonderful thing about being a Catholic is that church attendance does not need to stop when you go on vacation. I wrote earlier about the family vacation in which we travelled with our car full of children from our home north of Toronto to the southern tip of the Grand Canyon, camping along the way. Since our lives are highly structured and busy all year long, we have established a tradition of *laissez-faire*, unplanned vacations that make many of our friends cringe. We don't always know where we will be from one day to the next, let alone each Sunday. On this particular trip, we found ourselves in Albuquerque, New Mexico, on the first Sunday of our vacation. We marched off to the church in the middle of town – San Felipe de Neri. This beautiful adobe church had been established by Franciscan missionaries in 1706. Being there was like being transported back in time to a small Spanish village. We entered the church. It was so full that our family could not sit together. We divided into three groups. But we knew the prayers; we knew when to sit and when to stand; we knew the songs. Although we were thousands of miles from home in a 300-year-old church, we were home. We belonged. We were with family.

> We both continue to attend church regularly wherever we travel to throughout the world. After many years of marriage, we are now able to share our faith together.—Trevor & Judy Lewis

The next weekend, we were camping in Yellowstone National Park. On Saturday night, we Googled "Roman Catholic churches" only to find that the nearest one was three hours away. On Sunday morning, we were prepared to read the Sunday readings as a family and acknowledge that we might not be able to perfectly fulfill our Sunday obligation that week. However, as we packed up our wet tent and drove to the park office, we decided to ask if there was a Catholic church nearby that didn't show up on Google. Lo and behold, the Jesuits (an order of priests and religious brothers founded by St. Ignatius of Loyola) have a mission to Yellowstone. Every Sunday, a Jesuit priest comes to the park and celebrates the Eucharist with campers. We were told Mass was scheduled to begin in twenty minutes in the lodge just up the road. We drove up, joined with about thirty other wet and muddy campers, and set up chairs and tables to transform the lodge into a makeshift chapel. We began Mass. We knew the prayers; we knew when to sit and when to stand; we knew the songs. Although still thousands of miles from home, we found a home – this time in a ten-minute-old "church." We belonged. We were with family.

And *this* is *your* family. Wherever you go, you have a home in the Catholic Church. Even when the Mass is in a different language, the format and the words are the same. You can count on knowing the prayers, knowing when to sit and stand, and (most of the time) knowing the songs.

As you worship with your universal family, you will encounter liturgies that are wonderful and familiar. But in the Church, we also advocate inculturation. That means we encourage people to bring their local customs and traditions into the liturgy[9] and the practice of the faith. In my own travels, I have seen beautiful examples of such inculturation. Once when we attended Mass in a Vietnamese parish, the liturgical ministers, ministers of hospitality (ushers), ministers of the Word (lectors) and extraordinary ministers of Holy Communion all wore a simplified version of traditional Vietnamese dress. Outside the church, a small canteen sold spring rolls and other Vietnamese foods. After Mass, about a third of the congregation stayed for a small feast, and some money was raised to help with the upkeep of the church. Although we didn't understand the language, we *did* understand the liturgy. We still met Christ in the Eucharist and in the community gathered to share in it. It truly is wonderful to belong to such a large and united yet diverse family.

As you pray with your Catholic family in places other than your parish, some experiences may not inspire and uplift you. As our family has travelled the highways and byways and attended Sunday Mass in various towns, we have experienced both beautiful expressions of our faith and terrible preaching, painfully bad liturgical music and unfriendly congregations. Not everyone has the talent or the resources or even the inclination to provide the best that the Church has to offer. Nevertheless, as we pray in these circumstances, we still meet Christ in the Eucharist and in the community gathered to share in it. (Often, we come home with a far better appreciation for the preaching and music and hospitality in our home parish.)

PRACTICAL SUGGESTIONS

Attend Mass every single week.

Attend Mass while you are on vacation.

Prepare for Sunday Mass by reading the readings ahead of time. You can subscribe to the Living with Christ missalette (if you prefer reading from books) or download the Living with Christ app for your smartphone (if you like a digital version).

If you are unable to attend Mass because you are ill, take part in a televised Mass or watch one online, or read over the readings of the day using a smartphone app.

If you are seriously ill and cannot attend Mass, call the parish and have Communion brought to you. If you are in the hospital, speak to the nursing station or hospital chaplaincy department to arrange for someone to bring you Communion.

Find a way to be more involved in Sunday Mass – be a lector, an extraordinary minister of Holy Communion, or a minister of hospitality, or join the art and environment committee.

Sit in the same place every week so you get to know a few people well.

Sit in a different place every week so you get to know a variety of people. People are very consistent about where they sit in church. Changing seats can be almost like changing parishes in some cases.

Don't be afraid to let people know you are a new Catholic. Ask them questions when you don't understand. Most people genuinely love to help.

Learn all you can about the Mass. Many good YouTube videos are available to walk you through the Mass step by step. It is likely that what you have been taught about the Mass thus far has only scratched the surface of what you could learn.

Ask for a tour of your parish church. Learning about the significance of the building, the furnishings and the items used at Mass can deepen your experience of prayer during the Sunday worship.

Attend weekday Mass. Expect a quieter, shorter service that is quite different in tone than Sunday, though the same in structure.

The Gift of Sabbath

While placing Sunday Eucharist at the centre of our prayer life is vital, it is supported by the larger practice of keeping the Sabbath – or honouring the "Lord's Day." Slowing down is essential to keeping our sanity – as well as our faith – in this culture. We live in a world that has an unhealthy, maybe even idolatrous, love of busy-ness, efficiency and action. Human beings have never been so averse to stillness as they are in today's dominant culture. The high level of stress-related illnesses (both physical and psychological) shows that this busy-ness affects us negatively.

> Sometimes our family's schedule of activities and sports make it a challenge to come to church, but we always found a way. The great thing about church is that it is always there for you. It is a weekly reminder for me to pause, reflect and appreciate everything.—Brooke Shortt

Nothing natural functions without rest. All animals (including humans) rest. All animals play. Rest is not simply good, it is essential. That is why in the Hebrew Scriptures (Old Testament), resting is not a suggestion: it is a commandment. It bears the same weight as do not steal and do not kill. In the words of Scripture scholar Walter Brueggemann, "YHWH is a Sabbath-keeping God, a fact which ensures that restfulness and not restlessness is at the center of life."[10] This is echoed in more colloquial terms by writer Anne Lamott, who wrote that "almost everything will work again if you unplug it for a few minutes, including you."[11]

God undoubtedly foresaw the age of the internet. God knew that even with a clear commandment at the beginning of the Ten Commandments, we would have a hard time finding any dormant time with Snapchat, Facebook, Instagram, Twitter and other social media. The Sabbath commandment tells us to slow down, regenerate, enjoy the company of our family and friends. It calls us to be more reflective and observe God's action in our lives. Sabbath keeps us from being slaves. It reminds us that we do not live to work. Rather, we work to live.

Other cycles of rest and work and celebration can be found in the Jewish tradition out of which our faith grows. These came in sets of seven. Ron Rolheiser articulates it well:

> Biblically, this is the pattern: We're meant to work for six days, then have a one-day sabbatical; work for seven years and have a one-year sabbatical; work for seven times seven years (forty-nine years) and have a jubilee year; and finally work for a lifetime and have an eternity of sabbatical. The idea is that our pressured, hurried, working days should be regularly punctured by times of rest, celebration, enjoyment, non-work, non-pressure, and that ultimately all work will cease and we will have nothing to do except to luxuriate in life itself.[12]

Sounds appealing, does it? It is indeed. Sabbath is a wise, time-tested manner of structuring our lives.

> GO TO CHURCH! Sitting in the same pew allows you to make pew buddies! Familiarity makes you feel at home. As one of our initiation team leaders said, "I am going to church on Sunday; the only decision to make is what time!"—Laurie O'Heir

In our family, although our children sometimes groaned about getting up on Sunday mornings for Mass, they always obeyed the command to refrain from working on Sundays. They knew the whole "Sabbath thing" came as a package. Beds were not made, toys were not picked up, floors were not swept. (Setting the table and washing the dishes were the only exceptions to this.) As a result, Sundays were a low-key, family-centred day.

In previous times, the culture not only supported Mass attendance, it also supported a day of rest. Stores were closed on Sunday and no employer worth their salt would dream of expecting their employees to work that day. As with church attendance, this is no longer the case, and it is now up to us to make a conscious decision to structure Sabbath rest into our lives. From personal experience, I know this can be difficult.

Not long ago, I decided that I needed to get in shape, so I signed up our family for membership at the gym. One day, I was at the gym alone on the treadmill. I am admittedly terrible at doing nothing. Being on the treadmill felt to me like doing nothing, so I decided I would read a book at the same time. I chose to read Walter Brueggemann's book *Sabbath as Resistance*. In it, he argues that people today need to stop multitasking and rest. I realized that this might be a direct challenge to me in this very moment. As I was rationalizing my actions as not the sort of thing to which the author was referring, I stopped paying attention to my pace. I plummeted to the floor. Well, it felt like a plummet. I only fell a few inches. My hip was bruised but my pride was bruised even more when several people rushed over to see if I was hurt. Sometimes, the Lord has to give us a little push to get us to pay attention to what is fairly direct communication to us.

So, if you want to keep the faith (and stay on the treadmill), slow down. Rest! Keep the Sabbath!

PRACTICAL SUGGESTIONS

Keep Sundays special in as many ways as possible.

Limit the amount of work you do on Sundays.

Spend time with family and friends.

Have a Sunday dinner (in which everyone cooks and cleans up so that everyone also gets to rest).

Try not to shop on Sundays.

Celebrate the Rhythms of the Seasons

In the daily, weekly and annual cycles of the Church, all time is measured and celebrated so that we have a healthy balance of work and rest, action and contemplation, preparation and celebration.

The Church celebrates the annual cycle of time through the liturgical year. In the liturgical year, all of the most important sacred stories are told. It is a year-long spiritual journey through the life of Christ. We begin by placing ourselves with the people awaiting a Messiah. Then we stand before the newborn Christ at Bethlehem, honour him with the wise men, and so on through the events of his life. The climax of the liturgical year comes when we stand as witnesses to Christ's crucifixion and resurrection, receiving, as with the first disciples, the gift of the Holy Spirit so we can join them in the mission of building the reign of God. The stories you have learned over the past year you will hear again and again until you know them by heart. They are stories with such significance that one telling will simply not do. Over time, they will mould you and shape you more and more into a disciple of Christ. They will eventually become your story as they are interwoven into the events of your life.

The Church's celebration of the liturgical year hallows (makes holy) all of our time. Even the term "Ordinary Time" means counted time. Every moment is counted. Every moment matters.

As you make a few trips around the liturgical year as a Catholic, you will find that in our prayers and rituals, we also honour the seasons of the natural world. Remember that for Catholics, creation reveals the Creator. Thus, for us, the seasons are sacramental. They have a cosmic significance. For instance, in the death of the natural world in winter and its restoration to life in spring, we see a hint of our own death and resurrection, won for us by Jesus.

> I cannot believe how emotional I get at Easter. Easter never meant anything to me before I joined the Church.—Laurie O'Heir

When you joined the Church, you committed yourself to following a different calendar than that followed by the secular world. We do not begin our year on January 1st but four weeks before Christmas, with the first Sunday of Advent. Observing the liturgical year can help us remember that we are called as Christians to live in a way that will always be out of sync with the world around us. We are not inherently opposed to the world. It has been created by God and is good. But neither are we one with it. We are here to transform it so that it becomes more clearly the reign of justice and peace that God intended it to be. This means that sometimes we must choose to live differently. Sometimes we must protest that which is not holy, good and just. Sometimes we must be out of sync. Following a different calendar can train us for that.

As you adopt the rhythms, moods and traditions of the liturgical year, your faith will find an anchor. You will be reminded of the events of Christ's life upon which you are called to model your own. Your appreciation and understanding of the stories of Scripture and the tales of God's holy people will grow and deepen with each retelling.

PRACTICAL SUGGESTIONS

Purchase a liturgical calendar for your home.

Learn about the traditions of Advent, Christmas and Epiphany, and Lent, Easter and Pentecost.

Use an Advent wreath and an Advent calendar to help you mark the weeks and days of Advent.

Celebrate the traditional twelve days of Christmas, ending with a house blessing on the feast of the kings (Epiphany).

Spend Advent waiting for Christmas, not celebrating it. Hold off on Christmas carols, lights and celebrations until as close to Christmas as possible.

Prepare for Easter by joining in the forty-day period of Lenten preparation.

Celebrate Easter for the full fifty days. (Forty days of fasting and fifty days of feasting is not the best diet plan, but it is a clear message that joy trumps sadness.)

Attend the Easter Triduum services – Holy Thursday, Good Friday, Holy Saturday.

Attend the Easter Vigil. You may not have realized it when you made your baptismal vows to God before the community at Easter, but you will have the chance to renew these again and again, as all Catholics renew our baptismal promises every year at Easter.

Find out how people of different cultures celebrate the liturgical seasons and incorporate some of these traditions in your own life.

Discover and celebrate the feasts of the saints in the liturgical calendar.

Learn more about the Jewish and Christian practice of sabbaticals and jubilees. Maybe you want to incorporate these into your life in some way.

Find out about the Catholic traditions of food and drink associated with the liturgical year.

Learn about the meaning of the liturgical colours used in the church and consider using them in your own seasonal decorating.

Lessons from Funerals

If you haven't had the opportunity to do so, attend a Catholic funeral or two. This may seem like strange advice, but the Catholic funeral liturgy was likely not covered in depth during your catechetical sessions. In a well-celebrated funeral, you will learn important things about what we believe as Catholics. If you pay close attention, you will notice that the funeral of a Catholic is not about the person who has died (just as the wedding of a Catholic couple is not about that couple). As Bishop Robert Barron often says, "Your life is not about you." Our funerals are celebrations of God's gift of eternal life to all who would receive it. Our weddings communicate our belief that the love of human beings hints at and attempts to imitate Christ's love for the Church. Our whole life is about God's plan for humankind to live in unity, peace and communion with God and one another. Ultimately, we are reminded of this when the priest says at the end of the funeral Mass, "May every mark of affection and every gesture of friendship that you give to others be a sign of God's peace for you."[13]

In our faith tradition, we all come before God as equals – in love, in repentance, in celebration and in death. The same funeral liturgy is prayed with only minimal variations over both prime ministers and homeless people. As a pastoral minister in a parish, I sometimes attend the funerals of people who have no family or friends. Only the priest, the deceased and I are present. Thankfully, this does not happen often. But here is the good news. For the person who dies with not a friend on earth, the Church still prays the same prayers and proclaims the same Good News of eternal life as if the Church was filled to overflowing. And that person is still surrounded by all the saints and angels. With our eyes closed, we will not be able to tell the difference between the funeral of a prince and that of a pauper.

The symbols of the funeral liturgy – a white garment (pall), incense, prayers to saints, the Paschal candle[14] – are declarations of our Easter faith. They remind us that ultimately what we chose when we chose this faith is the promise of eternal life. In the words of poet Robert Bly, "even in death you're safe."[15] The more deeply we understand this, the more profoundly we will value our faith.

PRACTICAL SUGGESTIONS

Attend a Catholic funeral. Anyone can attend any funeral. You do not need to know someone to pray for them.

Visit a cemetery and pray for the dead.

Learn how Catholics in general (as well as in specific cultures) ritualize our passing from this life to the next.

If someone close to you dies, you may ask to have their name mentioned in the Prayer of the Faithful at Mass. You may also have a Mass offered to pray for them.

Pray for those who have died.

4

CONNECT WITH THE CHRISTIAN COMMUNITY

Stubbornly Communitarian

Thomas Merton, a well-known Catholic monk and writer, once wrote, "It is a glorious destiny to be a member of the human race, though it is a race dedicated to many absurdities and one which makes many terrible mistakes: yet, with all that, God Himself gloried in becoming a member of the human race. A member of the human race!"[16] We are, indeed, blessed to be members of this community into which God chose to dwell. We are also blessed to be given the gift of each other.

One thing about Catholics that will become apparent to you, if it is not already, is that we are stubbornly communitarian. We believe profoundly in the power and wisdom, indeed the necessity, of banding together as companions on this journey of life.

This is why when you are baptized, you are assigned a sponsor to support you. We do not believe it is possible for people to be healthy in isolation. We believe even more strongly that it is not possible to be a whole and healthy

Christian in isolation. We need companions. The word "companion," in fact, means those who break bread together.

> What helped me grow in faith was the support from my family and friends. The fact the Church brought us together as a community reinforced my faith and commitment to the teachings. Once confirmed into the faith, I had many discussions with friends about our faith, and I was able to impart historical and modern views and revive some aspects of the faith that they took for granted and/or had forgotten.—Ann Chrustie

For Catholics, being companions is not simply about supporting one another. It is much more significant. We believe that when we gather together, we become the Body of Christ. Just as we teach that when you hear the Word of God and when you receive the Eucharist you are truly meeting Christ, we also teach that when we encounter our brothers and sisters, we encounter the face of Christ.

> I exchanged phone numbers and Facebook information with my peers in the group. This was nice because we would coordinate to meet and go to church together on Sundays.—Kristen Garrity

We meet this presence of Christ most completely when our Church reflects the fullness of the human community. The Roman Catholic Church claims to be and strives to be a universal Church. The word "Catholic" comes from the Greek words *kata* and *holos*, meaning "for the whole." Irish writer James Joyce once described the Catholic Church as "here comes everybody." Thus, at most celebrations of the Eucharist, you will find babies and seniors, rich and poor, and people from a wide variety of cultures. (The latter, of course, depends on cultural diversity in the area where you live.) It is probably fair to say that Catholicism is the world's most diverse religious community.

Sunday worship is supposed to be a place where all are welcome, as a popular hymn by that name written by Marty Haugen declares. This means we must make a place for every person regardless of age, gender, culture or any other specific of human existence. In the Church, even "the outcast and the stranger bear the image of God's face."[17]

> My husband and I are blessed to have faith, as life throws a lot of curves at you and faith is the only thing to hold on to sometimes. Open your heart and mind to the preaching of the Church and the Gospel. Meet the people in your church, and find out what projects or committees appeal to you and know that even a small volunteer commitment is always very helpful.
> —Lynda O'Brien

This diversity is a marvellous gift. If you are open to it, your encounters with the many faces of Christ in your community can lead you to deeper knowledge of Christ himself and bring you wisdom and insight. People from cultures and demographics different from your own can help you see the world in ways that you cannot if you only meet people who are like you. Engagement with people who are different from you can take you out of yourself in much the same way a pilgrimage does. They can help you to look at your life from a different vantage point. St. Thomas Aquinas taught that this diversity of humanity (and of all creation) is necessary because no single creature can adequately reflect the perfection of God. He writes that God "brought things into being in order that his goodness might be communicated to creatures and be represented by them; and because his goodness could not be adequately represented by one creature alone. He produced many and diverse creatures, that what was wanting to one in the representation of the divine goodness might be supplied by another."[18] As a new Catholic, embrace this diversity... for you are now part of it.

Know also that you have your own unique and important contribution to make to the Church as a new Catholic. You have the potential to notice things that regular Catholics take for granted. You can help remind us of the wisdom and the beauty of our faith. And you bring particular insights to us that come from your experiences before you joined the Church. Do not be afraid to bring that which you learned as a Lutheran or Muslim or non-religious person. You have chosen this Church because something here attracted you and because you have met Jesus here. That does not have to mean, however, that you leave everything from your former life behind. From your past as a Lutheran, you might bring your knowledge and deep love of Scripture. From your past as a Muslim, you might bring your commitment to prayer. From your past as a non-believer, you might bring your questioning heart. The Catholic Church will be enriched by your contribution.

The "catholic" nature of the Church, however, also brings some challenges. You will find yourself in the pews with people who look, act and think differently than you. If you take your faith seriously, you will have to work together with them to build God's reign in your parish, in your community and in the world. This will sometimes be a challenge. It is certainly easier to belong to a group of like-minded people, but that will not provide the same opportunity for spiritual, emotional or personal growth. Take full advantage of this diversity to help you grow in knowledge and holiness.

In the Church you will find people who are socially and politically conservative and socially and politically liberal. Dorothy Day and Mother Teresa sat on opposite ends of the political spectrum, but both were Catholics in good standing with the Church. Both were also impressive examples of Christian discipleship.

The life Jesus calls us to live will never find complete correspondence in any political party or social movement. Some in the Church might want you to believe otherwise. Do not allow yourself to be pulled into the scandal of division. Despite what you might hear in some circles, the Roman Catholic Church is not a conservative institution. Nor is it a liberal institution. It is a group of people who attempt to follow Jesus Christ. As such, we are always going to be countercultural. What we counter in any given culture will vary according to the culture. Our duty is to celebrate and encourage what we see in our society that corresponds to the teaching of Christ. It is also our duty to call out the de-humanizing, immoral and harmful elements of our society. We do this best by living as Jesus' disciples. People have always been inspired more by actions than by words. And society is less likely to hear our condemnation than to be moved by the witness of our lives.

Our faith calls us to be engaged in the world. We not only *may* but we *must* bring our values and commitments to the public arena. However, if we follow Christ first – rather than a political ideology – we will always stand before the ballot box feeling conflicted. The choices offered will always be imperfect. As you learn how to live this faith in the public sphere, talk to your brothers and sisters in Christ about how their faith informs their decisions. Learn from the wide variety of Catholics how to do the difficult work of putting faith into action.

> After RCIA I wanted to continue to be a part of that close group and the wider church community; and I wanted to continue learning and growing in the wisdom and knowledge of Christ. After RCIA, Mass became even more important to me, as I better understood what was said, why it was said, and I felt that I could participate more, and be a part of the Mass. It made Mass more meaningful.
>
> One might not have the regular company of your fellow catechumens and sponsors after the sacraments of initiation, but it is important to keep contact with them and to surround yourself with members of the Church who are close and will be there to support you and help you grow.—Angella Graham

Another instance where you will experience Catholic inclusivity is in the intergenerational nature of our worship. You may be surprised to see young children included in Sunday worship. Catholics do not send our children to

Sunday school or provide babysitting for them during Mass. North American culture tends to separate into groups by age. The Church does not do this. When we gather to pray and celebrate Christ's Presence, we want to include everyone. So, if you are a parent of small children, bring them to church. Sometimes, they may make some noise. But the Church is pro-life and pro-family at its core. When my own children were small, my husband and I brought the five of them to church every Sunday... and we didn't hide in the back of the church. We sat in the second pew from the front. We suspected that from time to time a few people were unimpressed with the wiggling and noise in our seat. But my husband always said, "I sit up front because I hope that for every one person judging us, there are four or five praying for us." Never think that you cannot attend Mass because your children might be disruptive. They likely will disturb others, and that is okay. Jesus welcomed children.

As a new Catholic, embrace the communal nature of the Church. If you want your faith to take hold, you will need the support of others. The sponsor you were given at your Baptism is meant to be a help to you. But they also signify the larger Christian community. Do not be afraid to seek the advice, information and companionship that other parishioners can offer. The bonds of co-operation and friendship you form will be important in helping you live up to your commitment.

PRACTICAL SUGGESTIONS

Make an effort to meet people in your parish.

Join parish groups – the Knights of Columbus, the Catholic Women's League, the Society of St. Vincent de Paul, the youth group, the prayer group.

Attend parish social functions – dances, picnics, bazaars.

Stick around after Mass and chat with people.

Intentionally talk to people who are different from you.

Participate in discussion groups where you can hear from people with a wide variety of opinions. Try to hear the wisdom in each person's perspective.

Share your thoughts, insights and opinions with others.

Tell people about your background, why you chose to join the Church, what you find interesting, beautiful and true, and what you still find confusing or difficult to accept.

Find a spiritual soulmate with whom you can openly share your spiritual life. The stories of the saints have many examples of sacred friendships (for instance, that between St. John of the Cross and St. Teresa of Avila).

Do not limit your experience of the Roman Catholic Church to the parish church in your hometown. Visit other parishes. Attend Mass at the cathedral. Acquaint yourself with the various expressions of Catholicism.

Immerse yourself in the age-inclusive world of
Catholicism. Give an understanding smile to the parents
of a disruptive toddler. Fetch the walker of an elderly
person. Do both at the same Mass if you can.

Make the Acquaintance of the Saints

As you begin to connect with the great variety of people
and expressions of the faith in the Catholic Church, it will
become abundantly clear that this is a community that
spans the globe. However, this *universal* Church not only
transcends geography and culture, it also transcends time.
When you became Catholic, you joined a "great cloud of
witnesses" who have lived in ages past but are with us still.
We call this the communion of saints. All these "holy men
and women" (as we sing in the Litany of the Saints at the
Easter Vigil) are here to help you.

The saints help in two important ways. They can pray
for you. Just as we ask our friends to pray for us, we can ask
the saints to pray for us. Death does not destroy the bonds
that we have as brothers and sisters in Christ who support
each other in our Christian lives. So, ask for the prayers of
the saint-friends with whom you connect, just as you would
ask for prayers from living friends.

The saints can also guide you, advise you, instruct you
and inspire you. Learning the stories of their lives and reading their writings can help you understand God's action
in your own life. The saints are real people with unique
personalities who faced their own specific obstacles in their
attempts to follow Christ. They come from every walk of
life – teachers, priests, labourers, physicians and artists. The

saints are young and old, rich and poor, healthy and infirm. They reflect the diversity inherent in the people of God. No matter who you are, you can find saints with whom you can connect.

> I have gone on many weekend retreats over the years. This plus learning about the saints and their great works has inspired me to want to be better, work harder and has given me a desire to help more.
> —Gary Marston

As you read the lives of the saints and as you meet people in the Church who inspire you, keep this in mind. Even if it appears that holiness comes easily to them, that is never the case. Every person has a story of struggle. Holiness is hard for everyone – even if it is not obvious on the outside. This is a good time to take the advice of writer Anne Lamott, who wrote this in a Facebook post on her 61st birthday: "Everyone is screwed up, broken, clingy and scared, even the people who seem to have it more or less together. They are much more like you than you would believe. So, try not to compare your insides to their outsides."[19] This is good advice for all of us. We're all a bit of a mess – even the saints, even the people in the Church who appear to find it easy to be loving, kind and holy. That is why we need each other. Even more, that is why we need Jesus. He was sent to help us get out of our messes and to be holier tomorrow than we are today.

PRACTICAL SUGGESTIONS

Read the lives and writings of the saints.

Watch movies about the lives of the saints.

Find out who your patron saint is and ask them to pray for you. (A saint can be your patron because they share your birthday or name or simply because you choose them as your patron.)

Learn about other holy people who may not be "official" saints, but who inspire you and teach you something.

Get to know the wise ones in your parish, especially the elderly members who have a lifetime of experience in following Christ.

A Field Hospital for Sinners

In your parish and in the global Church, you will find people who will inspire you with their sanctity, kindness, sense of justice and faithfulness. Seek out these people. Look to them for inspiration. As a community of believers, we bring the presence of Christ to one another. In many ways, we support each other through great tragedy and join together to increase our joy in times of blessing. But we do it imperfectly. That cannot be denied. When I teach about Church, I often say, only half-jokingly, that when Jesus said, "Wherever two or three are gathered in my name, I am in their midst," his followers perhaps forgot to record a second phrase, which was "and there are going to be issues." This is the plight of human gatherings, and the Church, though aiming for a higher standard, is not exempt.

Please do not be discouraged when you discover, and you *will* discover, that we as a Church are like your family. Like all families, we have a few dysfunctions. Sooner or later these will become visible to you. As you become more involved in your parish community, you will encounter greediness, pettiness, jealousy. You will experience exclusion and infighting. You will witness egoism and people who are trying to build their own small kingdoms instead of co-operating to build God's kingdom. You will observe people bickering over the use of pots and pans in the parish centre and wonder if they even have a clue about who Jesus is and how he calls us to act. Perhaps you will be astonished to witness these kinds of behaviours, hoping, rather, that the people in this wonderful parish you have joined really know how to act as followers of Christ. The thing is, they probably mostly do; they just forget when space in the parish centre or a prominent role in the liturgy is at stake. Try to be patient with them when you see un-Christian behaviour. For it is likely that these folks will also see a little un-Christian behaviour in you, too, from time to time.

> Having a mentor during the RCIA program helped a lot. It gave me someone I knew to talk to each week until I met others and after the process was over. One other major thing that helped me was joining the Knights of Columbus. Joining a ministry or some part of the active Church to solidify your being there helps a lot.—Dean Yeats

I once had an experience that helped me learn not to judge the bad behaviour of others too hastily. I was at a rummage sale at St. James–Bond United Church in Toronto. (Yes, that really was the name. St. James United and Bond United churches had amalgamated.) I had been observing the minister engage with the people. He was warm and welcoming and managed to invite many people to attend worship on Sunday without ever being pushy or making people uncomfortable. I was impressed. As I waited in line to pay for my purchases, I was considering approaching him to discuss collaborating with our church. I had been in a reverie about the possibilities when, all of a sudden, I found myself face to face with the minister, his hand stretched out to shake mine. It was unexpected. I hadn't mentally composed my script yet. So, when he said, "Welcome to St. James. Please join us for worship on Sunday!" I replied, "Highly unlikely!" Yikes! That came out all wrong! I struggled to recover, explaining, "I'm Catholic." Worse. Now he thinks that because I am Catholic, I would never darken the doors of his church, except to buy old junk. I had *meant* to say that as a person ministering in a Catholic church, "I'm occupied on a Sunday morning, but I would love to get together and talk about how we could collaborate on something. I like your style." But I conveyed entirely the opposite message. I became so embarrassed by the way I had miscommunicated that I just left abruptly. Once I recovered from my feelings of humiliation, I wondered to myself how often such a thing happens – that what is heard is the very opposite of what the speaker intended. That single encounter many years ago has stayed in the front of my consciousness and helped me to give difficult or offensive people the benefit of the doubt ever since. Perhaps it can help you, too.

I have also found it helpful to heed the words of Josémaria Escrivá, founder of Opus Dei, who said, "Don't say, 'That person bothers me.' Think: 'That person sanctifies me.'"[20] Each member of the Body of Christ has been given to us by God to help us grow in holiness and love. When we are irritated by someone's behaviour, we can grow in patience and tolerance. We can be called to love more deeply. At the very least, difficult people can remind us how *not* to act.

Pope Francis likes to remind Catholics that the Church is not a "museum of saints," but rather "a field hospital for sinners." None of us can hang up a sign outside our house that says "No sinners live here." We go to church because we are in need of healing. We need the support and guidance of our community. We also need the grace of God that is given to us in the sacraments and communicated to us in the Word. We don't come to church because we are holier than others, but because we want to become holier than we currently are.

I have always loved the term "practising Catholic." In truth, most of the time it is used it has a holier-than-thou context – as in, "Well, she's not a *practising* Catholic." But the term ought to communicate humility. It is an admission of our failure to get it right. We still need more practice. We are not *there* yet. Paradoxically, the better we become at something, the more often we practise. A concert pianist practises far more than a ten-year-old boy taking piano lessons for the first time. A professional hockey player practises more frequently than a fifteen-year-old girl playing house league games in her hometown. As we approach a level of expertise in an area, we find our desire, and perhaps our need to practise increases rather than decreases.

You do not need to dig deeply into the Church to find evidence that we are a pilgrim people. We strive for holiness, inclusivity, justice and righteousness, but we only partially achieve these things. We are on our way. As I mentioned earlier, the Christian community will fail you. It will sometimes fail you in shocking, appalling ways. You may even have to face the questions of outsiders and be embarrassed to admit that you willingly joined this community. When instances of abuse, racism, sexism and tyranny rear their ugly heads, know that they are not the Church. They are an aberration of what we are called to be. For these times, we ought to be contrite and repentant. We must speak out strongly against such reprehensible behaviour. Most importantly, we must protect those who are harmed by people in positions of authority in the Church. Nevertheless, even when the Church fails in substantial ways, we continue to believe in the promise of Christ Jesus, that even the "gates of hell" will not prevail against us. (Matthew 16:18) The Holy Spirit is with us – inspiring and guiding us. We are a pilgrim Church on a journey to holiness. Not quite there. At times, far away from our destination. Nonetheless, we are pointed in the direction of the kingdom of God.

PRACTICAL SUGGESTIONS

Try your hardest to give people the benefit of the doubt. Most of the time, most people, even when hurtful, act with good intention.

Pray for the members of your parish community, and ask them to pray for you.

Pray for persecuted Christians.

Pray for your enemies.

Pray for the Church.

As you read the newspaper, pray for those who are suffering and pray in gratitude for those who are doing good in the world.

Speak up when you feel the parish or larger Church is not acting as it ought to act.

When We Fail

One thing that can happen – to new and old Catholics alike – is that people stop practising their faith when they have a lapse in faithfulness or when they experience a life-sized catastrophe. Maybe they've missed Mass for a few weeks. Or their marriage has fallen apart. Or their child has developed an addiction. Or they have developed an addiction. Or they've just become too busy and put their faith on the back burner for a while. I've watched people experience all these scenarios, and sometimes it causes them to stop practising their faith. They feel they have failed to live up to the vision they chose, and they are embarrassed to return. If this happens to you, be assured that you are not alone, even if you may feel you are. Many of the people sitting in the pews have been where you are now.

You will inevitably fail to live up to your baptismal promises. Everyone does from time to time, including many of the saints. You will have times of doubt, of spiritual laziness, of moral failure. Faith in God and the practice of that faith will ebb and flow. At times, you will feel your commitment strongly and live it faithfully. At other times, the opposite will be true. Do not be discouraged. The Church is a community of second chances. It is a Church whose founder chose St. Peter – the man who denied him three times – to be its first leader. It is a Church who calls Thomas – the man who wouldn't believe the Risen Lord until he could place his hands in the wounds in Jesus' side – a saint.

> Knowing that God is with me every day, listens and forgives me for my many faults, sustains me in my faith. Going to Mass every week and knowing that God and the Church will help you through the good times and the bad gives you strength you didn't know you had.—Debbie Teuma-Castelletti

If you feel that you have failed to fully practise the faith, the Church offers a wonderful solution – the sacrament of Reconciliation. You may also have heard it called Confession or Penance. Ultimately, we believe so strongly in the God of Second Chances that we have a full sacrament devoted to celebrating God's forgiveness and reconciliation. In most parishes, a weekly time is allotted for Confession as well as periodic gatherings where the whole parish gathers to celebrate the sacrament. It is common to find such communal gatherings taking place during Advent and Lent. Priests are always available to hear your confession individually outside of scheduled times.

If you are serious about spiritual growth, you will want to regularly take stock of how you do and do not live up to your calling to love God and neighbour. We call this examining your conscience. It is likely you will find yourself called to repentance in one area or another. It is even more likely that you will need to hear a word of forgiveness spoken and to be told that you are loved and accepted regardless of your sin. Do not be embarrassed by your weaknesses. Everyone in the Church is in the same boat. In fact, so is everyone in the human race.

PRACTICAL SUGGESTIONS

Attend services of reconciliation during Advent and Lent.

Go to confession not only when you have failed in significant ways, but also to confess the small ways in which you have been unfaithful. It is the small but unattended offences which cause the breakdown of most relationships.

Examine your conscience regularly and ask God for forgiveness and help to overcome the temptations you face in your life.

Ask God to help you forgive those who have hurt you.

5

PUT FAITH INTO PRACTICE

Become Very Good at Washing Feet

The ultimate test of our faith is found in our good works. If we love God, we must love our neighbour. The two are bound together inextricably. So, if you want your faith to last a lifetime, it cannot just be something you believe. It must also be something you do. The goodness that we do in the world as persons of faith actually builds up our faith and helps us to maintain it. So teaches St. Peter:

> For this very reason, you must make every effort to support your faith with goodness, and goodness with knowledge, and knowledge with self-control, and self-control with endurance, and endurance with godliness, and godliness with mutual affection, and mutual affection with love. For if these things are yours and are increasing among you, they keep you from being ineffective and unfruitful in the knowledge of our Lord Jesus Christ. (2 Peter 1:5-8)

At the Last Supper, Jesus taught his followers what it means to be a disciple. First, he prayed with them. Then he ate with them. After that, he washed their feet. The disciples were shocked and perhaps appalled. This was not how leaders behaved. But Jesus was clear: "If I, your Lord and Teacher, have washed your feet, you also ought to wash one another's feet. For I have set you an example, that you also should do as I have done to you." (John 13:14-15)

If we are to be disciples of Jesus, we also must become good at washing people's feet.

> When I finished RCIA, I wish someone had given me an *Integration Manifesto* on how to get involved! In my case, I responded to an offer to become a lector and that has led to an ever-growing and firmer commitment to the life of the Church and service to its members. Someone recognized a gift of the Spirit in me and called on me to use it in the service of the Church. Speak to other members and find out what your gift is and find a place to serve where that gift is a blessing to others in the Body of Christ.—Joanne Barnett

The people who have most successfully connected with the Church have almost all become involved in some sort of service. They have signed up to proclaim the Word as lectors or to welcome people at the doors of the church as ministers of hospitality. They have become involved in the Society of St. Vincent de Paul so that their lives might make a difference to the poor, or they have offered to help make sandwiches for funeral luncheons so they may lighten the burdens of the grieving. They have offered to use their engineering expertise to retrofit the church's lighting to make it more earth-friendly. The Catholic Church is a life-affirming, justice-building tradition. Your unique talents can be engaged in endless ways.

In feeding the hungry and giving drink to the thirsty, in clothing the naked and visiting the imprisoned, in engaging in all the works of mercy which Jesus explicitly tells us to do, we find our salvation. (Matthew 25:31-46) We also find our purpose here on earth. That purpose is centred on participating in God's plan for humanity. That plan includes building a reign of justice and peace where all God's children live in freedom, love and righteousness. The more mature our faith becomes, the more it will become a faith that reaches out in service. Service is one of the non-negotiables of Christian life.

Ambassadors of Christ

> When I had completed the RCIA program, I was also honoured to be able to volunteer with the Grade 8 Confirmation process that again reinforced my understanding and commitment to my faith and impart it to the students. I also joined a Bible study with a group of friends. As well, I sponsored my friend into the faith, and she has flourished as a faithful elementary teacher and it has had a very positive impact on her life.—Ann Chrustie

This story has been told from more than one pulpit. A man was in a hurry to get home after a long and difficult day of work. Let's call him Tim. Because Tim was in a bad mood, he had been driving aggressively, though not illegally. He had yelled out the window at other drivers and might even have raised a middle finger at one or two of them. After one such instance, Tim was surprised to see the flashing light of a police car in the rear-view mirror. "Great!! This is all I need," he thought.

When the officer came to his window, Tim asked, confused, "What did I do, officer?" then added, "I'm sure I didn't do anything illegal."

"No," said the officer, "nothing illegal, but I was thinking that possibly you were driving a stolen car."

"A stolen car?" asked Tim, puzzled.

"Yes," said the officer, "when I saw the bumper sticker on the back of your car that said you belonged to St. Mary's Church, and I watched how you were driving, I figured there's no way a good Catholic would be so inconsiderate and rude. The driver of that car must have stolen it."

Now that you are a member of the Church, you are an ambassador. What you say and do becomes to the world what the Church says and does. When one part of the Body is injured, the whole Body hurts. When one part of the Body sins, the whole Body is judged. This is one reason why the sinful behaviour of some Church leaders is such a scandal.

While it is possible that God has called you to be a great and famous saint, it is not likely. You are probably called, as are the bulk of Christians, to everyday holiness. Do not underestimate the importance of this role. You've probably heard critics of the Church declare that the reason they don't belong is because "All the churchgoers I know are hypocrites" or "They think they are better than everyone else" or any other number of things. In reality, these folks probably experienced one or two people who bore these sinful traits. Nevertheless, they generalize their experience to the entire Church. This is wrong and unfair. But it happens… often. Of course, we cannot be on our best behaviour all the time, but we can take seriously our responsibility to be ambassadors of the Church and thus ambassadors of Christ. (2 Corinthians 5:20) We can be the Church we wish to see.

It is not easy to be good. We do not always want to do what Christ calls us to do. But we are called to do our best. And doing good even when we do not want to do good has a transformative effect on us. The more we make the practice of kindness, gentleness and patience part of our daily living, the easier it becomes. We become good by doing good. We become better people with every kind action and positive moral choice we make. As St. Francis de Sales taught: "You learn to study by studying, to play on the lute by playing, to dance by dancing, to swim by swimming. So also learn to love God and our neighbour *by loving* them, and those who attempt any other method are mistaken."[21]

Following Christ to the Cross

American Catholic writer Flannery O'Connor once wrote, "What people don't realize is how much religion costs. They think faith is a big electric blanket, when, of course, it is the cross."[22]

This Church that you have joined is not for the faint of heart. While the Church will at times be of great comfort to you in your sorrow and pain, it will also be the place where you will be challenged to love your enemies and pray for those who persecute you. It will be the place where you will be asked to give up everything you have and give it to the poor.

If we as a Church are doing our job, you will hear messages from the pulpit that make you squirm in your seat. When we proclaim the Scriptures, we speak prophetic words. As a community, we have a striking ability to be oblivious to the challenge of the Word of God. Thus, writer Annie Dillard asks, "Does anyone have the foggiest idea what sort of power we so blithely invoke? Or, as I suspect, does no one believe a word of it? The churches are children playing on the floor with their chemistry sets, mixing up a batch of TNT to kill a Sunday morning. It is madness to wear ladies' straw hats and velvet hats to church; we should all be wearing crash helmets. Ushers should issue life preservers and signal flares; they should lash us to our pews."[23]

Christianity is about following Christ to the cross. As Father Daniel Berrigan wrote, "If you intend to follow Jesus, you had better look good on wood."[24] We have been promised that the yoke of Christ is easy and his burden light. But there *is* a yoke and a burden. We will have God's ever-present, abiding help all the way. We will also have brothers and sisters in Christ to stand in solidarity with us and to pray for us. And that's a good thing, because we will need it.

In many places in the world, to be a Christian is to risk one's life. However, if you live in most parts of the Western world, persecution is likely to be subtle. It will consist of people at the office thinking you are strange for believing what you do. There will be comments – sometimes intended for you, sometimes not. But there will be times, in the workplace, in the family, in the community, where the call to stand up for what you believe will involve great risk. You may lose friends, jobs, opportunities or more. This is when your faith will be tested. But you will have the prayer of the

Church, the examples of saints and martyrs and the support of the community, as well as the strength of the Holy Spirit that was given to you in Confirmation. These will help you when the call to live the Gospel becomes most difficult.

Faith that Permeates Life

> If you have just joined the Church, be patient with your faith journey, ask questions and join programs that the Church offers. For me, attending my marriage preparation program and sacramental preparation programs for my children were helpful.—Brooke Shortt

The faith of Jesus Christ was never meant to be practised on only one day of the week. It must be lived in the marketplace, in the family, in society. It is a faith that should touch and transform every area of our lives, from the thoughts we think in secret to the way we vote in elections. If we reduce the practice of our faith to something private – just between us and God – or if we restrict it to something done on Sunday to remind us to "be a nice person" on Monday, then sooner or later, it will wither. You can read a good book from the Oprah Book Club and accomplish that much.

Faith that lasts a lifetime is much more significant. It is eyes that see God everywhere. It is a mind that calls us to right thought and right action every hour of every day. It is hands that communicate love and healing to everyone we meet. The faith that lasts a lifetime is a faith that permeates our entire being and becomes so much a part of us that we cannot imagine living any other way.

PRACTICAL SUGGESTIONS

Participate in Lenten and Christmas charitable initiatives.

Support the parish financially. When we do our part for the parish, we make it our own.

Find a way to help the poorest and neediest people.

Serve food at a community meal.

Learn about the corporal and spiritual works of mercy. Practise them often – daily, if possible.

Be a conscientious consumer. Pay attention to how and where the products you buy are made.

Buy locally made products or products that support individual families whenever you can.

Live simply and consume less.

Be conscious of how your life affects God's creation.

Practise random acts of kindness and senseless acts of beauty – as the bumper sticker says.

Learn about Catholic Social Teaching.

Find out about Catholic organizations that work to transform the world: pro-life groups, Development and Peace, Catholic Worker, Pax Christi, L'Arche.

Bring questions of faith to the ballot box. The Church often publishes guides for voters at election time.

6

ONGOING FAITH FORMATION
AND DEVELOPMENT

For your faith to be a living faith, it must be fed. It must grow and develop and mature. This takes a lifetime. The Church, however, provides a treasure trove of resources and supports.

Acquaint Yourself with the Great Thinkers and Artists of Catholicism

Reading and writing are not just for school. They can also be valuable tools for prayer, reflection and ongoing spiritual growth. The thoughts of others, whether spiritual reflection, poetry or fiction, can lead us to deeper insights about what it means to be a follower of Jesus in this Roman Catholic tradition. Fiction especially can provide you with a way to immerse yourself in the Catholic worldview. While you are still new to the faith, reading Catholic writers can help develop your sense of the perspectives and sensibilities of this community to which you have been called to belong. Read some of the writers listed below. This is just a small taste of a great banquet of offerings. You will not like them all, but the more you read, the more you will learn just what it means to belong to a Church that calls itself "universal."

> Twenty-five years later, I'm still trying to understand everything.—Gary Marston

- ▸ **Christian Classics of Spirituality:** With 2,000 years of history, there are countless options. For starters try *The Confessions* of St. Augustine, *Revelations of Divine Love* by Julian of Norwich, *Dark Night of the Soul* by St. John of the Cross, and *Spiritual Exercises* of St. Ignatius.
- ▸ **Contemporary Catholic Writers:** Visit any reasonably well-stocked Catholic bookstore and you will find more than you can read in a lifetime. Try Father Ron Rolheiser, Bishop Robert Barron, Sister Joan Chittister, C.S. Lewis, Father Henri Nouwen, Jean Vanier, Father James Martin, Matthew Kelly, Father Thomas Merton, St. Josémaria Escrivá or Dorothy Day.
- ▸ **Novelists:** The following novelists will give you a good taste of the world and worldview of Catholics: David Adams Richards, Flannery O'Connor, J.R.R. Tolkien, C.S. Lewis, Graham Greene, G.K. Chesterton, Evelyn Waugh, James Joyce and Frank McCourt.
- ▸ **Poets:** Try Gerard Manley Hopkins, Denise Levertov, Sor Juana Inés de la Cruz, Hilaire Belloc or Blessed John Henry Newman. The prayers of saints such as Thomas Aquinas and Augustine also qualify as poetry.
- ▸ **Artists:** Since art is a central way in which Catholics embody theology, it is almost impossible to name only a few artists. Search online for Catholic artists. Do not limit yourself to famous Europeans. Use qualifiers such as

"Canadian, contemporary, modern, ancient, Indigenous, African, Asian," etc. to help you find images that you might not otherwise find. Some of my personal favourites are Georges Rouault, Michael O'Brien, Leland Bell, Sister Corita Kent, Ade Bethune and William Kurelek.

Your spiritual growth can be aided not only by reading the writings of others, but by writing your own reflections. Journalling, which was earlier presented as a form of prayer, can also be a helpful way to chronicle and assess your spiritual development. It can provide a way to look back over time and consider how you have grown (or not) in your relationship with God.

Explore the Great Traditions of Spirituality

As you pursue your Catholic life, you may also want to explore the many great traditions of spirituality in the Church. A spiritual tradition is characterized by prayer styles and charisms (gifts) such as hospitality, prayer or service to the poor. Such a spirituality is based on the writings or example of a holy person (often a saint) and is typically lived out in a religious community. However, their practices can also be fruitful for lay people. Some religious orders even have formal organizations of lay people associated with them.

Once you have learned the basics of Catholicism, you may want to explore some of these varied traditions of spirituality. Some of the better known ones are Ignatian or Jesuit, Carmelite, Franciscan, Vincentian and Benedictine. As well, many contemporary spiritualities have been of great help to people; they range greatly in perspective from feminist and ecological spiritualities to Opus Dei.

Read the writings of the founders of these movements. Go on a retreat run by the religious orders that follow these spiritual traditions. You may discover a way of praying and practising your faith that compels you.

Embrace Change

If you want to keep the faith and grow in it, you will need to learn to embrace change. This may seem like strange advice given in the context of the Roman Catholic Church – sometimes regarded as the epitome of unchangeability. After all, this *is* a community of people who pray prayers that are more than 2,000 years old. "Blessed are You, Lord God of all Creation" is an ancient Jewish blessing prayer that existed long before Jesus. "The Lord be with you" was a greeting spoken at the time of Jesus' great-great-great-grandmother, and we still greet each other that way in church today. Every day in every country we celebrate Mass repeating the same story and using the exact words that Jesus used at the Last Supper: "Do this in memory of me." Perhaps because we belong to a Church that honours tradition so deeply, we are more resistant to change than others. As a new Catholic, you might not be as set on doing things "the way they have always been done." However, the unchanging nature of Catholicism is likely at least part of the reason you were attracted to this Church.

Not only does everything that is not God fail to be perfect, but everything that is not God also changes. Only God is unchanging. Change, however, seems to make most of humankind uncomfortable, if not outright angry. If a person's faith rests in something less than God, then sometimes change can rock one's faith.

In the parish where you became Catholic, you probably like the priest, the community, the music or any number of other things. These aspects of your parish's expression of Catholicism have helped make the faith appealing to you. However, Catholic parishes change. We cannot depend on having the same priest, catechist, parishioners, music or even church building that first attracted us to the faith. The parish music director may quit, and the music ministry take on a different flavour. The priest may be moved to another parish, and parishioners will lament that the new pastor "is nice but just isn't the same." Art, music and social structures all support faith. But they can never replace faith in the Living God. They are temporary, impermanent. Only God is eternal.

One hallmark of Catholicism is to honour Tradition. We believe God is revealed in Scripture and in Tradition. The Church's understanding is that God's revelation in Tradition is unchanging. However, the great Tradition is passed down through many smaller traditions. We also honour tradition in this sense – the prayers, songs and rituals that have inspired the people of God for centuries, if not millennia. We do this, recognizing that change is also good. It is a sign of growth. Indeed, to pass on traditions without adding the marks of each new generation is to betray Tradition. For each age, each person has their own insights into the nature of God and faith. You can be confident that in this Church, change will not be marked by a flavour of the month. However, there *will* be change. It will be hard. But it will also help you to see things in new ways and challenge you to grow in ways that God intends for you.

In conclusion, if you want to keep the faith to the end, it is important to be patient with the imperfection and impermanence of all that is not God. All the gifts God gives can lead us to God, help us learn about God, and support us in our faith in God, but they cannot replace God. When they fail us, as they inevitably will, we need to be sure that our faith is first and foremost in God so that it remains intact.

Don't Take Yourself Too Seriously

Finally, if you want to live a lifetime of faithfulness, you will need to equip yourself with a healthy sense of humour, a robust appreciation of feasting, and a deep and abiding joyfulness. Six times the psalmist urges us to "make a joyful noise" before the Lord. St. Teresa of Avila is rumoured to have said, "From silly devotions and sour-faced saints, good Lord, deliver us." In the same spirit, Hilaire Belloc wrote:

Wherever the Catholic sun doth shine,
There's always laughter and good red wine.
At least I've always found it so.
Benedicamus Domino![25]

Humility dictates that we do not take ourselves too seriously. Catholics, in general, know how to laugh at ourselves, although you will inevitably meet some exceptions. For years, the Catholic parish was the place to go for a good game of Bingo, and you can even find Catholic board games such as *Is the Pope Catholic?* Dom Pérignon was created by a French Benedictine monk. Almost every Catholic saint's feast is associated with food or dance. Need I even mention St. Patrick's Day? Joy is God's desire for all of us. Life is a gift, meant to be savoured.

PRACTICAL SUGGESTIONS

Explore spiritual direction. A spiritual director is a professionally trained person who helps to guide others in their spiritual development. In the past, only priests and nuns had spiritual directors, but it is becoming much more common for lay people to seek the advice of a sage and professional guide to the spiritual life.

Subscribe to a few Catholic blogs. Ask someone in leadership in your parish for advice about good ones to follow.

Join a Catholic book club at your church. If there isn't one, start one.

Take advantage of adult education opportunities offered in your parish or diocese.

Watch educational videos about the Church, theology, the saints. Catholicism by Bishop Robert Barron is an excellent place to begin.

Watch films by Catholic filmmakers.

Learn about some of the spiritual traditions of the Church.

Enjoy life! Fast, yes, but feast more!

CONCLUSION

As a newly initiated Catholic, you have been through a year of intense learning, study and formation. It will take a while for this to sink in and for your understanding of your Catholic faith to develop. Although it may seem like you have learned a great deal, you have only just begun. You will continue to have many more questions. You will also have the opportunity to gain much more knowledge and wisdom. Learning to be a follower of Christ is the work of a lifetime. *Mystagogia* – opening up the mysteries – never ends.

Now that you no longer have your initiation team guiding you in learning about your faith, you will need to seek the support you need to continue to grow. Mine the depths and the breadth of this tradition. It has a wealth of riches to offer.

If you rest your faith in the abiding love of God – Father, Son and Holy Spirit – if you root yourself in prayer, most especially in Sunday Eucharist, if you immerse yourself in the Christian community, if you live a life of service and if you continue to feed your heart and soul, this faith of yours will flourish. This is what the Church hopes and prays for you.

We welcome you into this marvellous, beautiful (and sometimes frustratingly less than perfect) Church. We are grateful you count yourself to be one of us. We hope we can help you grow more deeply in your love of Christ and his people.

Keep the Faith!

ENDNOTES

1   "God Beyond All Praising" is a hymn written by Michael Perry in 1982 and published by Hope Publishing Company. It is sung to the tune of THAXTED by Gustav Holst.

2   "How Great Thou Art" is a hymn written by Carl Boberg in 1885.

3   Anne Lamott, *Help! Thanks! Wow! Three Essential Prayers* (New York: Penguin Random House, 2012), 1.

4   Second Vatican Council, *Sacrosanctum Concilium* (Constitution on the Sacred Liturgy), http://www.vatican.va.

5   "Be Not Afraid" is a popular Catholic hymn written by Bob Dufford, S.J. in 1975 and published by Oregon Catholic Press.

6   Julian of Norwich, *Revelations of Divine Love.* Translated by Elizabeth Spearing. Introduction by A.C. Spearing. (London: Penguin Classics, 1998), 7–8.

7   Gerard Manley Hopkins, "God's Grandeur," in *God's Grandeur and Other Poems* (Don Mills, ON: Dover Publications, 1995), 15.

8   Second Vatican Council, *Lumen Gentium* (Dogmatic Constitution on the Church), 11, http://www.vatican.va.

9   Since you are new to the faith, Catholic vocabulary may still be unfamiliar. The word "liturgy" literally means "the work of the people." Typically, the word refers to the Mass, but may also refer to other public and formal prayer celebrations in which Christians engage.

10 YHWH refers to the unpronounceable name of God revealed in the Hebrew Scriptures. Walter Brueggemann, *Sabbath as Resistance,* rev. ed. (Louisville, KY: Westminster John Knox Press, 2017), 10.

11 Anne Lamott, "Twelve Truths I Learned from Life and Writing," *TED Talks: Ideas Worth Spreading* (Vancouver, 2017), https://tinyurl.com/y72znvgw.

12 Ron Rolheiser, "Looking for Rest amid the Pressures of Life," November 26, 2006, https://tinyurl.com/ybrxutze.

13 Canadian Conference of Catholic Bishops, *Order of Christian Funerals* (Ottawa: CCCB Publications, 2016), 196.

14 The word "paschal" refers to the mystery of Christ's death and resurrection. The Paschal candle is the candle which is obtained anew each Easter and is placed in a prominent place in the church throughout the year.

15 Robert Bly, "People Like Us," in *Morning Poems* (New York: HarperCollins Publishers, 1998), 99.

16 Kathleen Deignan, ed., *Thomas Merton: A Book of Hours* (Notre Dame, IN: Sorin Books, 2007), 52.

17 Marty Haugen, "All Are Welcome" (Chicago: GIA Publications, 1994).

18 Thomas Aquinas, *Summa theologiae*. Translated by Fathers of the English Dominican Province, I.47.1. (New York: Cosimo Classics, 2007), 246.

19 Lamott, "Twelve Truths."

20 Josémaria Escrivá, *The Way* (New York: Doubleday, 1982), n. 174, p. 29.

21 Bishop Jean-Pierre Camus, *The Spirit of Saint Francis de Sales.* Translated by J.S. (Frankfurt: Outlook, 2018), 42.

22 Flannery O'Connor, *The Habit of Being: Letters of Flannery O'Connor.* Edited by Sally Fitzgerald (New York: Farrar, Straus and Giroux, 1988), 354.

23 Annie Dillard, *Teaching a Stone to Talk* (New York: Harper Collins, 198), 52.

24 Dan Berrigan, *To Dwell in Peace – An Autobiography* (Eugene, OR: Wipf & Stock, 1987), i.

25 Hilaire Belloc, "The Catholic Sun," https://allpoetry.com/The-Catholic-Sun.

MARQUIS

Québec, Canada